The Humanitarian Exit Dilemma

How should humanitarian organisations respond when their aid goes awry? Should they stay and remain engaged with the needy, or should they withdraw and leave? Investigating the choices involved and the judgements required when tackling these questions, this book explores the unique 'Humanitarian Exit Dilemma' that confronts humanitarian organisations.

Humanitarian practitioners often are too concerned with the outcome of action but fail to recognise that there are other equally weighty moral considerations they should consider. Focusing simply on the results of projects, such as the number of lives saved alone, is inadequate. To address this problem, this book highlights three value-based normative considerations, namely humanitarian aid workers' special relationships with those whom they are assisting, humanitarian organisations' causal responsibility to assist those they have made vulnerable, and humanitarian organisations' obligations to fulfil reasonable expectations of those assisted. Together, these three non-instrumental reasonings serve as the main arguments of the author's value-based normative account, the 'Non-Consequentialist Approach', to address the Humanitarian Exit Dilemma.

Offering a unique perspective on how humanitarian organisations should navigate the Humanitarian Exit Dilemma, this book will be of interest to scholars and practitioners in the field of Humanitarian Studies, African Studies, Refugee Studies, political philosophy, humanitarian action, and human rights.

Chin Ruamps is a Postdoctoral Research Fellow in the Department of Management, Society and Communication at Copenhagen Business School, Denmark. She is also a member of the Centre for Business and Development Studies.

Routledge Humanitarian Studies Series

Series editors: Alex de Waal, Dorothea Hilhorst, Annette Jansen and Mihir Bhatt
Editorial Board: Dennis Dijkzeul, Wendy Fenton, Kirsten Johnson, Julia Streets and Peter Walker

The Routledge Humanitarian Studies series in collaboration with the International Humanitarian Studies Association (IHSA) takes a comprehensive approach to the growing field of expertise that is humanitarian studies. This field is concerned with humanitarian crises caused by natural disaster, conflict or political instability and deals with the study of how humanitarian crises evolve, how they affect people and their institutions and societies, and the responses they trigger.

We invite book proposals that address, amongst other topics, questions of aid delivery, institutional aspects of service provision, the dynamics of rebel wars, state building after war, the international architecture of peacekeeping, the ways in which ordinary people continue to make a living throughout crises, and the effect of crises on gender relations.

This interdisciplinary series draws on and is relevant to a range of disciplines, including development studies, international relations, international law, anthropology, peace and conflict studies, public health and migration studies.

Child Rights in Humanitarian Crisis
Improving Action and Response
Edited by Rigmor Argren and Jessica Jonsson

The Humanitarian Exit Dilemma
The Moral Cost of Withdrawing Aid
Chin Ruamps

For more information about this series, please visit: www.routledge.com/Routledge-Humanitarian-Studies/book-series/RHS

The Humanitarian Exit Dilemma

The Moral Cost of Withdrawing Aid

Chin Ruamps

Routledge
Taylor & Francis Group

LONDON AND NEW YORK

Designed cover image: guvendemir

First published 2023
by Routledge
4 Park Square, Milton Park, Abingdon, Oxon OX14 4RN

and by Routledge
605 Third Avenue, New York, NY 10158

Routledge is an imprint of the Taylor & Francis Group, an informa business

© 2023 Chin Ruamps

British Library Cataloguing-in-Publication Data
A catalogue record for this book is available from the British Library

Library of Congress Cataloging-in-Publication Data
Names: Ruamps, Chin, author.
Title: The humanitarian exit dilemma : the moral cost of withdrawing aid / Chin Ruamps.
Description: New York : Routledge, 2023. |
Series: Routledge humanitarian studies series | Includes bibliographical references and index.
Identifiers: LCCN 2022059045 (print) | LCCN 2022059046 (ebook) | ISBN 9781032307954 (hardback) | ISBN 9781032307961 (paperback) | ISBN 9781003306696 (ebook)
Subjects: LCSH: Humanitarian assistance—Moral and ethical aspects. | International relief—Moral and ethical aspects.
Classification: LCC HV553 .R836 2023 (print) | LCC HV553 (ebook) | DDC 363.34/8—dc23/eng/20230308
LC record available at https://lccn.loc.gov/2022059045
LC ebook record available at https://lccn.loc.gov/2022059046

ISBN: 978-1-032-30795-4 (hbk)
ISBN: 978-1-032-30796-1 (pbk)
ISBN: 978-1-003-30669-6 (ebk)

DOI: 10.4324/9781003306696

Typeset in Times New Roman
by codeMantra

Dedicate to those who have shared splendid five years of time with me in Manchester at the greyest, rainiest time of my life.

Contents

Figures

Tables

Acknowledgements

I would like to extend thanks to the many people who so generously helped and supported me during the years in which this book has taken shape. Special mention goes to James Pattison and Stephen de Wijze. I am profoundly grateful for their tremendous support, and I thank James and Steve wholeheartedly.

Special mention goes to Ying-Tai Lung, Chi-Chen Wu, and Minn-Tsong Lin for nurturing my enthusiasm for political philosophy and public affairs.

Finally, but by no means least, thanks go to my partner, Mirko Ruamps and my family, Ying-Teng Lung and Li-Chen Chen, for their encouraging and long-lasting support. I am particularly indebted to my family for their constant faith in my work.

1 Introduction

Background

Due to the scale of humanitarian crises, relief aid and humanitarian resources have been allocated across disaster areas to help affected populations. International non-governmental organisations, such as humanitarian organisations, distribute essential goods such as food, shelter, and medical supplies to those badly affected by crises. According to the Global Humanitarian Assistance Reports, US$17.3 billion was contributed worldwide in response to humanitarian emergencies in 2012; contributions reached 76 million needy people. In 2013, US$20.5 billion was distributed to 78 million people. In 2014, expenditure on international humanitarian aid rose to a record high of US$24.5 billion in an attempt to assist 122 additional million people in need (GHA, 2013, 2014, 2015). About a decade later in 2020, the COVID-19 pandemic hit the world, intensifying existing needs and fuelling new crises resulting in an estimated 243.8 million people requiring humanitarian assistance (Thomas & Urquhart, 2020). Up until 2022, the COVID-19 pandemic continued to aggravate humanitarian needs with other pre-existing crises, affecting an estimated 306 million people across the globe (Girling & Urquhart, 2021).

However, needs resulting from the impacts of COVID-19 distract resources from other essential needs, leaving more affected populations hanging without vital support. This has further stretched the capacity of humanitarian organisations, which are facing morally difficult decisions in determining which needs to satisfy and on what grounds. On the one hand, humanitarian organisations have been tasked to address the needs of those suffering from man-made disasters such as conflicts and wars. During conflicts, affected populations are often forced to suffer inhuman and violent treatment such as involuntary

DOI: 10.4324/9781003306696-1

military recruitment, sexual abuse, and physical attacks (Milner, 2009; Mogire, 2006). The conflicts concentrated in the Gaza Strip in 2012, South Sudan in 2013, and Syria in 2014 highlight the troubling nature of humanitarian crises and the urgent need for international humanitarian assistance (GHA, 2013, 2014, 2015). On the other hand, natural disasters and epidemics drove needs to an unprecedented level. While climate-change-induced crises such as the tropical cyclone that hit Myanmar in 2008 and the devastating earthquake that struck Haiti in 2010 demonstrate the extreme scale of natural disasters (Bailey, 2014; GHA, 2013, 2014, 2015; OCHA, 2018), the COVID-19 pandemic has placed unprecedented pressure on humanitarian organisations.

Natural disasters, humanitarian crises, and man-made conflicts are often interrelated and correlated. Protracted natural disasters and long-winded epidemics often trigger political turmoil and economic collapse. Political and economic unsteadiness then leads to violent conflicts resulting in system failures (Kent & Burke, 2011). Weak institutional capacity, political instability, financial insecurity, population displacement, and fragile public infrastructure further escalate pre-existing conflicts, which often leads to failed states and complex humanitarian emergencies. For example, the unprecedented humanitarian need caused by the ongoing emergent conflict in Afghanistan in 2021 and Ukraine in 2022 has been intensified and exacerbated by the COVID-19 pandemic. Large-scale humanitarian needs and assistance call for urgent response and immediate humanitarian intervention: humanitarian organisations, state actors, and civil societies are motivated to enter disaster areas and engage in humanitarian missions for the purpose of saving lives and relieving suffering. However, humanitarian assistance and relief aid may cause more harm than good to affected populations, especially in complex emergencies.

Despite the fact that humanitarian assistance can alleviate suffering and save human lives, it can also exacerbate existing suffering and harm of the people it aims to help. For instance, humanitarian aid can relieve the burden of sustaining costly conflicts for warring parties (Hoffman & Weiss, 2006; Milner, 2009; Mogire, 2006; Terry, 2002; Weiss, 1999). However, the civil war in Nigeria in the late 1960s shows how humanitarian aid can also be misused: arm weapons were given under cover of humanitarian aid, while the belligerents played the refugee card to manipulate the public to provide more aid. The political violence in Cambodia in the 1980s illustrates a case where aid can do as much harm as good: humanitarian aid was forced to channel through the unjust regime, where aid was misappropriated and misused. Finally, in Rwanda in the 1990s aid was used by warring parties, armed combatants, to further extend the wars and conflicts. (Barber, 1997; Barnett, 2011; Boyd, 1995; De Waal, 1997; Landgren, 1995; Milner, 2009; Terry, 1999).

Humanitarian assistance can also bestow legitimacy on the authoritarian regime by cooperating with them (Lung, 2019). This is evident through the mass-scale persecution of the Rohingya people by the government of Myanmar. Since 2012, the government of Myanmar has placed tens of thousands of displaced Rohingya people in forced detention camps. To gain access and assist the Rohingya people, humanitarian organisations are forced to accept the enforced policy and remain silent about the harmful segregation policy in the fields. This has resulted in criticism of humanitarian organisations for being complicit in the Myanmar government's unfair segregation policies. Some humanitarian organisations decided to leave to avoid complicity in the segregation process. However, this has resulted in a lack of response and a shortage of resources for the large-scale needs of Rohingya refugees, which also causes moral uneasiness. In a sense, Rohingya refugees are left in the hands of the Myanmar military regime, with limited access to help and services. The Rohingya crisis in Myanmar poses a similar dilemma to the crisis in Tanzania in the 1990s. Rwandan refugee camps were set up in Tanzania following the 1994 Tutsi genocide in Rwanda. In both crises, humanitarian organisations faced the difficult question of whether to withdraw assistance to avoid the risk of becoming accomplices to the government's unethical political agenda or to remain engaged with those in need.

The civil war in Syria, especially after the rise of the Islamic State in 2014, further reveals how humanitarian assistance was controlled and used as a means by warring parties and armed combatants. The violence in Syria has displaced millions, forcing them to seek shelter in neighbouring countries. Despite the scale of the refugee crisis, international relief aid and humanitarian agencies have not been able to deliver effectively due to the extremely insecure context of the war. For example, humanitarian organisations were not granted access to the crisis-affected areas. Furthermore, humanitarian aid workers were abducted by warring parties as part of their political lobbying. The rising concerns for the safety of aid workers and ground operations amongst humanitarian organisations also limit the much-needed help.

The Taliban atrocity regime that gained complete control of Afghanistan in 2021 shows the paradoxical nature of humanitarian aid. The Taliban atrocities regime carried out indiscriminate attacks and intentional killings of civilians, journalists, rights activists, and humanitarian workers. What follows the Taliban atrocities regime's takeover of Afghanistan is the large-scale forced misplacement of Shia Hazaras people, the severe suppression of women's rights, and the collapse of the national healthcare system, further compromised by the COVID-19 pandemic. In view of the horrific events happening in Afghanistan, more and more humanitarian organisations are struggling between aborting operations to stop being complicit in the Taliban's unfair policy against women and remaining engaged in serving the needs of already-vulnerable female populations. In addition, the widespread famine caused by political turmoil and economic disruption in Afghanistan attracted great attention with an influx of humanitarian aid. Instead of distributing aid to starving civilians, the Taliban administration has used humanitarian aid to feed its close contacts, further reinforcing the political inequality in Afghanistan.

Overall, relief efforts and humanitarian assistance help save lives, protect rights, and provide much-needed essential goods to the affected populations. However, things get complicated when humanitarian organisations are forced to recognise the legitimacy of an unjust regime to gain access to the people in need, humanitarian resources are controlled by the warring parties to advance their political agendas, and aid workers are being held hostages in the game of political negotiation. In some other situations, relief aid can disrupt the local economy and further weaken the already fragile socio-economic system of the refugee-populated country.

To that extent, although humanitarian organisations can alleviate human suffering, the reality is that the humanitarian assistance provided sometimes increases the suffering of at least some affected populations. In view of this, some argue that humanitarian organisations' aims to alleviate suffering would be better served if they withdrew their resources to reallocate them elsewhere (Lischer, 2005; Pogge, 2007a, 2007b; Terry, 2002; Weiss & Collins, 2000). Others go so far as to suggest that humanitarian organisations' goals would be better served by not getting involved at all in the first place (Barber, 1997; Boyd, 1995).[1]

Although humanitarian organisations may reduce harm if they withdraw their resources to reallocate them elsewhere, there would obviously be a tremendous negative impact on affected populations if resources were withdrawn. They also fail to consider whether the provided resources have made the affected populations worse off (Ruamps, 2022). Moreover, emphasising maximising harm-reduction to reach the best outcome risks simplifying and ignoring other important values, which have various impacts on both humanitarian organisations and affected populations. However, this 'non-interference' perspective has its problems. Specifically, this perspective does not help humanitarian organisations answer the question of how to act once humanitarian organisations are already involved. Humanitarian organisations should address the further question of the status of withdrawing or staying when they are forced to face the Humanitarian Exit Dilemma. Thus, there is a need to take into account the potential harm befalling affected populations if aid is withdrawn for reallocation purposes.

Introduction

Humanitarian action brings hope and much-needed aid to the most vulnerable people affected by disasters. With the founding of the International Committee of the Red Cross (ICRC) in 1863 and the first treaty of the Geneva Convention of 1864 (ICRC, 1864),[2] humanitarian space was guaranteed by states and non-state actors, and belligerents were obliged to provide access to humanitarian actions (Hilhorst, 2002; Hoffman & Weiss, 2006).[3] Almost a hundred years after, with the development of the 1951 Refugee Convention and its 1967 Protocol, state governments came together to define the usage of the term refugee and outline the corresponding rights and the legal obligations to protect them.

Today there exist various initiatives that intend to protect vulnerable populations in extreme contexts of conflict and disaster. While legal frameworks such as International Humanitarian Law and International Refugee Law outline the responsibilities of states and non-state armed groups during conflicts and the rights of refugees, international guidelines such as the Sphere Humanitarian Charter, Code of Conduct for the Red Cross and Red Crescent Movement and NGOs in Disaster Relief, and the principles of the Humanitarian Accountability Partnership detail the accountable and ethical approach to respond to needs of people.

Since the late 1990s, warring parties have often not granted humanitarian non-governmental organisations (NGOs) sufficient space to provide humanitarian assistance. Humanitarian NGOs are repeatedly denied access to affected populations unless they cooperate or pay fees to unjust parties. Humanitarian workers are taken as hostages for armed combatants to realise their political ambitions. Finally, humanitarian aid is often misused and misappropriated for warring purposes. This negative manipulation of relief resources and international aid systems demands that humanitarian organisations reconsider their operations and practices in conflict settings. The challenges facing humanitarian organisations are no longer merely about shielding and sustaining affected populations. Instead, the new challenges have forced humanitarian organisations to confront unprecedented humanitarian dilemmas and ethical paradoxes, which require that humanitarian organisations respond to crises differently (Carens, 2007; Hoffman & Weiss, 2006; Lung, 2019).[4] Moreover, the shifting humanitarian space requires a 'humanitarian pluralism' that is more diversified in its approaches to affected populations and interpretations of principles of humanitarian action (Hilhorst, 2002; Hoffman & Weiss, 2006; Slim, 2015).

The shifting nature of conflicts—from international to local focus and from state armies to armed guerrillas and combatants—poses new challenges to humanitarian organisations. However, the fundamental humanitarian dilemma that confronts humanitarian organisations today remains the same. Regardless of who the actors are, when the conflict happens, and when the disaster outbreaks, humanitarian organisations are always forced to make a difficult choice that often involves an undesired moral trade-off. The choices involved and the judgements required in dealing with the seemingly new challenges are no different. It may be that a humanitarian organisation is forced to pull its on-the-ground aid workers out of a particular site due to extreme violence. It may also be that a humanitarian organisation has no choice but to withdraw its missions and exit because it no longer desires to be complicit in collaborating with the obvious wrongdoers (Lung, 2019).

There are different reasons why humanitarian organisations may want to withdraw and relocate their missions. Most of these are justified through calculating cost-effectiveness and overall best outcome. This is where things become problematic and morally questionable. With the utilitarian calculation in mind, a humanitarian organisation subconsciously emphasises to aid itself rather than the people in need. To be fair, a humanitarian organisation can rightly allocate and distribute much-needed resources in a way that can serve as many people as possible. And they should.

However, when other important normative values are at stake and are competing with this rationale of 'save the most', a humanitarian organisation may not be justified in ignoring all other equally important values. This book focuses on a very important aspect of humanitarian ethics and looks beyond the simple utilitarian approach to aid withdrawal, with a concept I refer to as the 'Humanitarian Exit Dilemma'. Hence, the central questions this book are concerned with: how should humanitarian organisations respond when their aid goes awry? Should they stay and remain engaged with vulnerable populations, or should they withdraw and leave? This book, in essence, addresses the question of withdrawing or staying when humanitarian organisations are forced to face the Humanitarian Exit Dilemma.

The central argument

The Humanitarian Exit Dilemma can manifest differently in a disaster setting, especially in conflicts and wars. As noted, humanitarian assistance and relief aid can relieve the burden of sustaining costly conflicts for belligerents (Barber, 1997; Lischer, 2005; Lung, 2019; Terry, 2002). It can also undermine local coping strategies as well as local economies and thus create victims' dependence on aid (Assal, 2008; Bartle, 2012; Christoplos, 2004; Devereux, 2004; De Waal, 1997; Hassan, 1996; Knack, 2000; Lung, 2019; Swift et al., 2002). Even so, humanitarian organisations' efforts are still typically *humanitarian*. To be more precise, humanitarian organisations are humanitarian in that they operate missions for the reasons of *humanity*.

Humanitarian practitioners often are too concerned with the outcome of an action but fail to recognise that there are other equally weighty moral considerations they should consider. Focusing simply on the results of projects, such as the number of lives saved alone, is inadequate. When humanitarian organisations disproportionately focus on outcomes that are measured in quantity than quality, their humanitarian efforts become no more than a "ritualistic search for quantifiable indicators", which leads to "meaningless evaluations" (Autesserre, 2014, p.241). In a sense, the current discourse of humanitarian assistance often starts "at the wrong end" because it always seeks what 'can' be measured rather than what 'should' be measured (Autesserre, 2014, p.242). Essentially, "counting the numbers does not decide the moral question", nor does numbers-counting help humanitarian organisations navigate their decisions when confronted with a moral dilemma (Timmermann, 2004, p.106).

We need a more developed account of humanitarian assistance to shed light on this matter. Therefore, the central aim of this book is to propose morally weighty non-consequentialist reasons for humanitarian organisations to remain engaged and continue their assistance.[5] In answering this question, this book offers a non-consequentialist account, which argues that humanitarian assistance is not simply about overall consequences but also other non-instrumental values. To that extent, the central claim is this: humanitarian organisations should act as consistently as possible with the non-instrumental values of *unique relationships, distinct dependence, and reasonable expectations.* I call this the 'Non-Consequentialist Approach' to the Humanitarian Exit Dilemma. Crucially, the 'Non-Consequentialist Approach' denies that the overall consequences (the maximisation of harm-reduction) *solely* determine humanitarian organisations' justification to stay or leave when they face the Humanitarian Exit Dilemma.

However, it does acknowledge that consequences can play an important role in determining the rightness of an action. Thus, the central aim of this book is to show that there are other important independent values in addition to concern for the maximisation of harm-reduction. This challenges humanitarian practitioners' usual practices, which often prioritise aid utility maximisation. During the decision-making process, humanitarian organisations too often consider the logic of consequences as the "best decision-making method to apply" and "any deviation from an ideal-typical consequential decision-making process was considered to be wrong" (Heyse, 2006, p.202). The aim of this book, then, is to move beyond this view and provide plausible humanitarian guidelines that humanitarian organisations could reasonably follow when facing the Humanitarian Exit Dilemma.

Scope of this book

This book delineates the most justifiable approach to tackling the Humanitarian Exit Dilemma by referring to literature on humanitarian assistance, applied ethics, and moral philosophy. This book focuses specifically on humanitarian organisations' decisions regarding aid allocation (i.e., withdrawing for reallocation purposes) when encountering the Humanitarian Exit Dilemma in disaster, especially in conflicts. Other ethical issues surrounding humanitarian organisations and their assistance are not the focus and will only be discussed briefly if necessary. Therefore, debates on the origin of humanitarian organisations, the expansion of humanitarian organisations, the diversity within humanitarian organisations, and the diversity of different humanitarian organisations are not considered explicitly. The following section delineates the scope of this book further by specifying (1) the kind of humanitarian assistance, (2) the sets of humanitarian organisations, (3) the types of moral dilemmas, and (4) the specific focus.

The kind of humanitarian assistance

This book focuses on relief aid and humanitarian assistance delivered *in extreme emergencies*. Obviously, extreme emergencies are more likely to result in sudden, large-scale, and unpredictable suffering that is much more urgent. Focusing on assistance provided in extreme emergencies is justified since "the more agendas for long-term change are incorporated into emergency response, the *less* it is distinguished by immediacy or escape from competing agendas and complex moral judgments" (Calhoun, 2008, p.25). Relief aid is, in general, one specific form of humanitarian aid that is delivered in the context of extreme emergencies. It represents a rapid response to a severe natural or man-made emergency that demands an immediate reaction to reduce suffering and casualties in the short term (Kopinak, 2013; Minear, 2002).

The reason for focusing on extreme emergencies, in particular, is because they provide the starkest circumstances in which the Humanitarian Exit Dilemma is present. In the case of development assistance, there is a far less pressing need, and the dilemma often does not arise or is not as severe, given the potential to soften the withdrawal of aid over the longer term. This book, therefore, is not concerned with the long-term agenda dedicated to economic development, poverty reduction, or peacebuilding. Nor does this book deal with projects promoting democracy or upholding human rights. Literature falling into such categories (such as literature on rehabilitation and development aid) is thus left aside.

In addition, this book does *not* distinguish between different kinds of man-made conflicts. For example, five main types of man-made conflicts can be identified depending on the cause, scale, intention, nature, and duration of conflicts (Fearon, 2004). While acknowledging that there are different kinds of man-made conflict, it is not within the scope of this book to make such a distinction.

That being said, there will be a discussion on the implication of the Non-Consequentialist Approach in other non-man-made disasters in the concluding chapter of this book. Although the main focus of this book is to shed light on the paradox of moral trade-offs prevalent in man-made disasters, it should be acknowledged that large-scale natural disasters often lead to violent conflicts and civil wars. Due to this, I will touch on what humanitarian organisations should do when facing a different but equally dilemmatic moral predicament in other non-man-made disasters by the end of this book.

The sets of humanitarian organisations discussed

This book focuses on particular sets of international non-governmental humanitarian organisations that mainly concentrate on relief aid and humanitarian assistance provisions in an emergency, such as ICRC, the Oxford Committee for Famine Relief (Oxfam), and Médecins Sans Frontières (MSF). Given the focus on the non-governmental and voluntary character of humanitarian organisations, the bilateral and multilateral aid that state actors, governments, or governmental organisations provide is not taken into account (Fast, 2014).

While the ICRC was formed to ensure all affected populations could access care based on the code of neutrality in Geneva in 1864, MSF was created in 1971, branching out from the ICRC. Bernard Kouchner, a doctor who was frustrated by delays in the Nigerian Government's approval for access to assist affected populations in Biafra and ICRC's code of neutrality, founded MSF (Shatz, 2002; Terry, 1999). Oxfam was founded in response to the mass-scale starvation in Greece in 1942. CARE was created after World War II and focused on providing aid to the affected population (Terry, 1999).

The humanitarian organisations listed above may profess different mandates. Some may profess a charitable duty to assist the most vulnerable, whereas others may base their action on the fundamental human rights of individuals by virtue of humanity. Nevertheless, they share certain important humanitarian features in common. These humanitarian organisations have the common objective of alleviating victims' suffering and prioritising the concern for humanity over other considerations (Carens, 2007; Terry, 1999). Most importantly, these humanitarian organisations all face the Humanitarian Exit Dilemma that agencies working exclusively on development projects would not face. This is because humanitarian organisations such as ICRC and MSF often perform humanitarian operations in the context of violence or insecurity, as opposed to development agencies (Barnett, 2011).

This is also because humanitarian organisations are often confronted with the Humanitarian Exit Dilemma due in large part to their commitment to humanitarian guiding principles, such as neutrality and impartiality, which is not the case for agencies working on development projects (Abu-Sada, 2012; Fast, 2014; Hilhorst, 2002). Even though some have started to engage in development work, they still emphasise emergency response compared to development projects (Barnett, 2011; Terry, 1999). Take MSF-Holland (MSF-H) as an example: according to MSF-H's Mid-Term Policy, the aim was to spend "65 percent of the budget on conflicts and emergencies, 25 percent on other medical humanitarian crises, and other 20 percent on unplanned emergencies" (Heyse, 2006, p.65).

The types of moral dilemmas in humanitarian action

International non-governmental humanitarian organisations often have different beliefs about crisis response, hold different expectations of humanitarian assistance, subscribe to different principles of humanitarian action, and endorse different ethical norms. They are *volitional* moral dilemmas, *cognitive* moral dilemmas, and *social* moral dilemmas (DuBois, 2008). While *volitional* moral dilemmas are dilemmas in which the agent knows what the right action is but is unsure if he or she can perform the action, *cognitive* moral dilemmas are dilemmas in which the actor is unsure about which action is the right choice to perform. In contrast to *volitional* and *cognitive* moral dilemmas, *social* moral dilemmas occur in cases where different actors disagree on what the right choice is (DuBois, 2008).

This book focuses on the Humanitarian Exit Dilemma of *cognitive* and *social* moral dilemmas. This suggests that humanitarian organisations are unsure about the right action and sometimes disagree about which action is right. It is worth noting that although this book focuses on the moral dilemma of humanitarian assistance in the conflict, I do not mean this to imply the 'dirty hands' approach to moral theorising. My point is that the quandary of aid is complex. I leave aside the case for and against 'dirty hands' reasoning in this book.

In addition, this book focuses on the specific ethical quandaries posed by the 'Humanitarian Exit dilemma'. Several humanitarian dilemmas are associated with humanitarian aid when given in the context of extreme emergencies. There are, for example, entry-assessment dilemmas, complicity dilemmas, speed versus quality dilemmas, localisation dilemmas, and exit dilemmas. Specifically, this book considers the exit dilemma, where the moral predicament arises when humanitarian organisations are forced to choose between withdrawing aid from the affected populations for the greater good and staying to continue assisting affected populations for certain weighty normative values.

The specific focus of this book

I now further specify the exact focus of this book and the particular question that I am interested in.

First, this book does not focus on making decisions between *two groups of symmetrical numbers of affected populations*. This book, instead, focuses on situations where humanitarian organisations have to choose between two groups of *asymmetrical numbers* of affected populations, on either the same or different timeframe in different places. Several cases that highlight the Humanitarian Exit Dilemma and the ethical predicaments that confront humanitarian organisations during the course of their operations are discussed in the course of this book, such as in Tanzania, Rwanda, the Democratic Republic of the Congo (DR Congo), Thailand, Nigeria, Uganda, Bhutan, Northern Mali, and the more recent cases in Myanmar, Syria, and Afghanistan.

I want to note that this book is a work of moral theory and political philosophy rather than sociology, anthropology, or ethnography. Hence, no interviews were involved, and no field research was conducted. Tanzania and some other countries are referred to using secondary resources as illuminating cases to help facilitate exposition and underpin arguments.

Next, as I have already alluded to above, this book considers situations where humanitarian organisations are *already* in the middle of their humanitarian operations and have been working in certain areas with particularly affected populations over a certain period. This book, therefore, does not look into questions such as whether humanitarian organisations should intervene and start their humanitarian missions *in the first place*.

Finally, this book does *not* compare all relevant factors that may contribute to the continuation of conflicts. Rather, specific interest lies in situations where aid is *highly likely* to prolong the conflict and intensify the existing suffering. In his recent research on humanitarian aid and civil war duration, Neil Narang (2015) argues that simply supplying aid to warring parties may not *necessarily* prolong the conflict. Narang finds that whether the aid provided to warring parties during the conflict will affect the duration of the conflict depends on whether the level of aid provided is easier or more difficult to estimate and observe by opponents (2015). This suggests that, although aid may prolong the conflict and intensify existing suffering in the context of conflict, the tendency for aid to prolong conflict lies mainly in its uncertainty and lack of predictability. In situations where the amount of aid is easier to observe and predict by opponents of the conflict, the higher the tendency is for aid to prolong the conflict.

Humanitarian aid, in this sense, can affect the "bargaining dynamics" between two opposing warring parties: the more aid one party receives, the lower its costs of fighting appear to be, and the less likely it is to collapse; the less likely it is to collapse, the more likely the conflict will be prolonged (Narang, 2015, p.187). This book does not consider situations where the provision of humanitarian assistance is not likely to prolong the conflict.

The 'Non-Consequentialist Approach'

I now outline my non-instrumental approach to the Humanitarian Exit Dilemma in more detail. Many theorists and aid practitioners have argued that humanitarian assistance should either be withdrawn or reallocated because aid can be counter-productive in humanitarian crises. This is based on the belief that overall humanitarian assistance has generated a more negative rather than positive impact on affected populations and that aid should be delivered in the most cost-effective way that can reduce harm and preserve more lives (Barber, 1997; Glennie, 2010; Lischer, 2005; Nunn & Qian, 2014; Pogge, 2007a, 2007b; Terry, 2002).

However, withdrawing aid eliminates the possibility for humanitarian organisations to save the specific lives of affected populations they are already helping. Although there are good reasons to think that relief aid exacerbates conflicts and generates more harm in the long run and should thus be withdrawn, humanitarian organisations may want to stay for other weighty moral reasons. In an attempt to shift the current humanitarian assistance discourse, which emphasises the maximisation of harm-reduction and lives preservation, I propose a 'Non-Consequentialist Approach' that highlights the moral significance of the non-instrumental values of special relationships, distinct dependence, and reasonable expectations.

The non-instrumental values of special relationships, distinct dependence, and reasonable expectations are briefly illustrated below, with an in-depth discussion in Chapters 3, 4, and 5, respectively. Chapter 2 shows the practical significance of the Humanitarian Exit Dilemma. In contrast, Chapter 6, the concluding chapter, draws together these three distinct non-instrumental accounts to offer a complete account of the Non-Consequentialist Approach.

First, the Non-Consequentialist Approach claims that humanitarian aid workers sometimes form a special relationship with those they are assisting. These special ties between the affected population and humanitarian aid workers, in turn, provide the affected population with an *additional claim* on humanitarian aid workers' attention and help. Common-sense morality seems to acknowledge that we owe special obligations to particular individuals if they stand in some special relation to us. To that extent, if humanitarian aid workers' particular action is detrimental to the well-being of those with whom they stand in special relationships, humanitarian aid workers should avoid performing such action. Therefore, humanitarian organisations should take humanitarian aid workers' special relationship with those they are assisting into account along with the concern for effectively delivering aid.

Second, evidence has shown that humanitarian assistance provided in conflict can severely undermine local coping capacities and the domestic economies of affected areas. This situation, in turn, makes aid recipients who are currently relying on aid even more vulnerable and more dependent on external assistance (Assal, 2008; Bartle, 2012; Christoplos, 2004; Devereux, 2004; Hassan, 1996; Knack, 2000; Swift et al., 2002). Although aid recipients currently relying on aid need external assistance, third parties, such as state actors, are often denied access to refugee-populated areas due to political disputes. This has made current aid recipients uniquely dependent on humanitarian organisations' assistance. Considering that humanitarian organisations are causally responsible for making current aid recipients so dependent and that current aid recipients are additionally vulnerable (due to the lack of help from other third parties), they bear an obligation to stay and remain engaged with aid recipients in question (Ruamps, 2022). Hence, the Non-Consequentialist Approach suggests that humanitarian organisations take the vulnerability of current aid recipients and the causal responsibility of humanitarian organisations' own actions into consideration when making decisions relevant to withdrawing and staying.

Third, some field reports have indicated that humanitarian organisations can mislead current aid recipients to form reasonable expectations of their continued assistance. For instance, current aid recipients can be led to expect humanitarian organisations' continued assistance if they have operated their humanitarian missions over a period of time on a regular basis. Current aid recipients can also be led to trust that humanitarian organisations will continue to care for them due to the kind of role and tasks humanitarian organisations voluntarily assume. Together, these two factors often induce current aid recipients' reasonable expectations of humanitarian organisations' continued assistance. However, humanitarian organisations could have exercised due care in some situations and taken reasonable precautions not to lead current aid recipients to expect their continued assistance but failed to do so. In situations where humanitarian organisations could have avoided creating current aid recipients' reasonable expectations, their culpable negligence has held them responsible for protecting current aid recipients from significant harm arising from unfulfilled expectations. This, in turn, requires humanitarian organisations to stay and remain engaged with the current aid recipients in question. Finally, I focus on a narrow consequentialist account of the response to the Humanitarian Exit Dilemma, which I call the 'simple account of consequentialism'. The simple account of consequentialism holds that all that matters is the maximisation of the utility of humanitarian assistance, which calculates costs and benefits only in terms of the overall utility of humanitarian aid and the number of people one can save. To put this another way, the focus of simple consequentialism is on efficacy and effectiveness in delivering humanitarian aid. Thus, I am not rejecting all accounts of consequentialism. The reason for such specific focus lies in that humanitarian organisations generally adopt the simple account of consequentialism when delivering aid, as suggested by several findings (Bolton, 1994; Hoffman & Weiss, 2006; Lischer, 2005; MSF Holland, 1994; MSF Speaking Out, 2014a, 2014b; Stockton, 2003; Terry, 2002; Terry & Cordaro, 1994).

Overall, the Non-Consequentialist Approach provides a non-instrumental account instead of the *simple* consequentialist account of 'saving the larger number'. In contrast to the simple account of consequentialism, the Non-Consequentialist Approach suggests humanitarian organisations focus on the source and the depth of their humanitarian commitments.

I should add a quick caveat here: as I discuss further in Chapter 6, this book focuses on repudiating the *simple* consequentialist account, which focuses on the efficacy of aid—how many lives will be saved. However, it might be that a more complex consequentialist account could take into account some of the values that I highlight. It is a moot point in moral philosophy whether agent-centred values can be incorporated within consequentialism, where they are subject to maximisation. This book hence is not concerned with this issue. For the purpose of the book, it simply needs to repudiate the simple consequentialist account, which overlooks the three non-instrumental values that this book highlights.

Book overview

I now provide a brief overview of the rest of the book. Chapter 2, 'The manifestation of Humanitarian Exit Dilemma', delineates the different ways the Humanitarian Exit Dilemma can manifest in the context of conflicts.[6] It considers the specific kinds of ethical predicaments that can arise in the face of the Humanitarian Exit Dilemma. After elaborating on how the Humanitarian Exit Dilemma can manifest in conflicts and the kinds of ethical predicaments that can arise, I use Tanzania as an illustrative example. I highlight how the Humanitarian Exit Dilemma manifested in the refugee crisis in Tanzania, the ethical predicaments that arose in Tanzania, and the decisions made. I also discuss the instances of the dilemma in Nigeria, DR Congo, and Cambodia. This chapter aims to explain the different ways that the dilemma arises and contextualise it with recent cases.

In Chapter 3, I start the defence of the Non-Consequentialist Approach. I focus on special relationships between humanitarian aid workers and the affected population. Humanitarian organisations should consider the moral significance of humanitarian aid workers' special relationships with the affected population once these relationships are formed. This is because the special relationship provides humanitarian aid workers with presumptive reasons to act and helps facilitate the overall aid effectiveness. Therefore, special relationships provide the first justification for humanitarian organisations to stay and remain engaged with the affected population in question.

In Chapter 4, I present the second major reason to stay instead of withdrawing humanitarian assistance. This chapter shows how humanitarian assistance can create current aid recipients' unique dependence on aid. Several findings and field reports are presented in support of this claim. Building on Scott M. James' 'Unique Dependence Argument', I present the 'Distinct Dependence Argument' to address the aid dependency predicament in the context of conflicts. This highlights the vulnerability of certain aid recipients and the causal responsibility of humanitarian organisations in making aid recipients dependent and thereby vulnerable.[7]

In Chapter 5, I highlight the moral importance of filling reasonable expectations. First, I discuss the differences between reasonable expectations and promising in the hope of providing a distinct 'Reasonable Expectation Account' that exclusively discusses reasonable expectations and their moral significance. I compare this account to Thomas Scanlon's 'Promissory Expectation Account'. Overall, Chapter 5 considers the normative strength of current aid recipients' reasonable expectations and humanitarian organisations' need to fulfil these expectations.

Finally, Chapter 6 provides a complete account of resolving the Humanitarian Exit Dilemma. Chapter 6 summarises the three non-instrumental accounts discussed in Chapters 3–5, as opposed to the simple account of consequentialism. More specifically, the three non-consequential values (Special Relationships, Distinct Dependence, and Reasonable Expectations) and a consequentialist concern for maximising harm-reduction are compared and weighed against each other. Drawing on this, I provide a set of modified principles of humanitarian action in an attempt to assist humanitarian organisations in their decision-making process when they face the Humanitarian Exit Dilemma. An implication section follows the end of Chapter 6, dedicated to the discussion on how the Non-consequentialist Account can be applied and help address other non-man-made disasters.

Contribution of this book

The original contribution of this book is straightforward. There has not been any detailed, sustained ethical analysis of whether humanitarian organisations should stay or withdraw when encountering the Humanitarian Exit Dilemma amid their operations. Much of the existing debates on the ethics of humanitarian action are underdeveloped normatively. Although there are many empirical works, the question of whether humanitarian assistance should withdraw or remain engaged when facing the Humanitarian Exit Dilemma and the entailed ethical predicaments is not fully explored. To that end, this book assesses all the potentially relevant normative considerations.

Humanitarian assistance is predominated by empirical accounts, which mostly suggest that humanitarian organisations withdraw their assistance given its apparent negative impact. Examples of aid's negative impact are ample: armed combatants have used refugee camps as safe zones to rest and recruit armed combatants (Lischer, 2005; Milner, 2009; Ruamps, 2022), and warring parties have gained the perceived legitimacy and right to rule because humanitarian organisations collaborate with them (Rieff, 2002; Ruamps, 2022; Terry, 2002; Weiss, 1999). Although this may be true, such criticisms say little about *humanitarian ethics* that underlie humanitarian assistance's fundamental values. It appeals to consequentialism to justify humanitarian action with aid effectiveness and the number of lives saved—but neglects important non-instrumental considerations. Considering this, this book intends to fill this pronounced gap, and, in particular, it does so by providing accounts of three aspects of humanitarian ethics. These are humanitarian aid workers' unique relationships with those they are helping, humanitarian organisations' causal responsibility to assist those they have made vulnerable, and humanitarian organisations' obligations to fulfil reasonable expectations of those assisted.

The aspects of the general normative force of unique relationships relevant to humanitarian assistance have remained underdeveloped.

The existing view on humanitarian assistance holds firmly that humanitarian organisations are agencies of professional occupations and should thus engage in humanitarian actions with professional ethics. However, such a view ignores that humanitarian organisations often rightly have agent-centred principles of their own and often perform humanitarian operations based on their agent-centred reasoning. In addition, humanitarian aid workers in the field may develop special ties with those they assist. There has been little or no acknowledgement in the humanitarian crisis that humanitarian aid workers' unique relationships and humanitarian organisations' agent-centred reasoning can be important.

The view that considers what causal responsibility one should bear when causing harm to others is also pertinent to humanitarian assistance. Whether humanitarian organisations have backwards-looking responsibilities, such as causation or blame, to current victims (dependent on aid) when aid is withdrawn and pulled out has not been adequately investigated. The existing opinion mainly considers the negative impact of humanitarian assistance and thus views the continuation of assistance as 'causing more harm'. Such a view fails to thoroughly consider the negative impact and harm caused by the withdrawal of aid. Nothing has been said about the harm caused by humanitarian organisations when they withdraw assistance: humanitarian organisations may be responsible for the harm befalling affected populations when they withdraw assistance because they can significantly contribute to affected populations' dependence on aid.

Finally, there has been no acknowledgement in humanitarian assistance that humanitarian organisations, just like individuals, can mislead people into forming reasonable expectations. The notion of reasonable expectation is not new. There are debates regarding one's obligation to those one has misled to form a reasonable expectation of his specific action. However, the aspects of reasonable expectation relevant to humanitarian assistance, similarly, are not discussed. Indeed, as this book argues, humanitarian organisations sometimes mislead victims to form reasonable expectations of their assistance. In doing so, this book highlights the moral relevance of reasonable expectations and trust.

Notes

1 An in-depth analysis of how the Humanitarian Exit Dilemma can manifest in conflicts and what corresponding ethical predicaments can arise are discussed in Chapter 2, using Tanzania as an example.

2 The first treaty of the Geneva Convention was the Convention for the Amelioration of the Condition of the Wounded in Armies in the Field, Geneva, 22 August 1864 (ICRC, 1864).

3 I use 'belligerents' as a broader term to include rebel groups, warring parties, militants, warlords, and insurgents.

4 The term 'victims' is used interchangeably with the terms 'aid dependents', 'aid recipients', 'affected populations' and 'refugees' throughout this book. This is because not all victims receiving humanitarian aid are refugees.

5 The best outcome here is the ability to reallocate aid to other places where more people can be helped (more lives can be preserved) and where aid will not generate negative impacts.

6 Chapter 2 has been published as an article. See Lung (2019) for the full article.

7 Chapter 4 has been published as an article. See Ruamps (2022) for the full article.

References

Abu-Sada, C. (2012). In the eyes of others: How people in crises perceive humanitarian aid. *Médecins Sans Frontières-USA (MSF-USA)*.

Assal, M. A. M. (2008). Is it the fault of NGOs alone? Aid and dependency in Eastern Sudan. *Sudan Working Paper, 5*, 19.

Autesserre, S. (2014). *Peaceland conflict: Resolution and the everyday politics of international intervention*. Cambridge: Cambridge University Press.

Bailey, S. (2014). Humanitarian crises, emergency preparedness and response: the role of business and the private sector: a strategy and options analysis of Haiti. *HPG (ODI), Humanitarian Futures Programme*. https://www.unocha.org/sites/unocha/files/HAITI%20case%20study%20FINAL.pdf

Barber, B. (1997). Feeding refugees, or war? The dilemma of humanitarian aid. *Foreign Affairs, 76*(4), 8–14.

Barnett, M. (2011). *The empire of humanity: A history of humanitarianism*. Ithaca, NY: Cornell University Press.

Bartle, P. (2012). *The dependency syndrome*. [Community Empowerment Collective]. Retrieved from http://cec.vcn.bc.ca/cmp/modules/pd-dep.htm

Bolton, S. (1994). *Press and Tanzania/Rwanda crisis*. International Press Officer for East Africa. Retrieved from http://speakingout.msf.org/en/node/436

Boyd, C. (1995). Making peace with the guilty. *Foreign Affairs, 74*(5), 22–38.

Calhoun, C. (2008). The imperative to reduce suffering: Charity, progress, and emergencies in the field of humanitarian action. In *Humanitarianism in question: Politics, power, ethics* (pp. 73–97).

Carens, J. (2007). The problem of doing good in a world that isn't: Reflections on the ethical challenges facing INGOs. In D. Bell & J. Coicaud (Eds.), *Ethics in action* (pp. 257–272). Cambridge: Cambridge University Press.

Christoplos, I. (2004). Out of step? Agricultural policy and Afghan livelihood. *Afghan Research and Evaluation Unit, Issue Paper Series*, 1-78.

20   *Introduction*

Devereux, S. (2004). *Proceeding from UNOCHA '2005: Food security issues in Ethiopia: Comparisons and contrasts between lowland and highland areas.* Addis Ababa: Pastoralist Communication Initiative.

De Waal, A. (1997). *Famine crimes: Politics and the disaster relief industry in Africa.* Oxford: James Currey.

DuBois, J. M. (2008). *Ethics in mental health research: Principles, guidance, cases.* New York: Oxford University Press.

Fast, L. (2014). *Aid in danger: The perils and promise of humanitarianism.* Philadelphia: University of Pennsylvania Press.

Fearon, J. (2004). Why do some civil wars last so much longer than others? *Journal of Peace Research, 41*(3), 275.

Girling, F., & Urquhart, A. (2021). Global humanitarian assistance report 2021. *Development Initiatives.*

Glennie, J. (2010). More aid is not the answer. *The Journal of Contemporary World Affairs, 109*(727), 205.

Hassan, A. A. (1996). Beyond the locality: Urban centres, agricultural schemes, the state and NGOs. In L. Manger, H. Abd el-Ati, S. Harir, K. Krzywinski & O. R. Vetaas (Eds.), *Survival on meagre resources: Hadendowa pastoralism in the Red Sea hills* (pp.103- 119). Uppsala: The Nordic Africa Institute.

Heyse, L. (2006). *Choosing the lesser evil: Understanding decision making in humanitarian aid NGOs.* Aldershot: Ashgate Publishing Limited.

Hilhorst, D. (2002). Being good at doing good? Quality and accountability of humanitarian NGOs. *Disasters, 26*(3), 193–212.

Hoffman, P., & Weiss, T. G. (2006). *Sword & salve: Confronting new wars and humanitarian crises.* Lanham, MD: Rowman & Littlefield.

ICRC. (1864). *Convention for the amelioration of the condition of the wounded in armies in the field.* Geneva, 22 August 1864 [Data file]. Retrieved from https://ihl-databases.icrc.org/ihl/INTRO/120?OpenDocument

Kent, R., & Burke, J. (2011). Commercial and humanitarian engagement in crisis contexts: current trends, future drivers. *Humanitarian Futures Programme,* King's College London, UK. http://www.humanitarianfu-tures.org/wp-content/uploads/2013/06/Commercial-and-Humanitarian-Engagement-in-Crisis-Contexts-HFP-20111.pdf

Knack, S. (2000). *Aid dependence and the quality of governance: A cross-country empirical analysis.* Washington, DC: World Bank.

Kopinak, J. K. (2013). Humanitarian aid: Are effectiveness and sustainability impossible dreams? *The Journal of Humanitarian Assistance, 10*, 1–25.

Landgren, K. (1995). Safety zones and international protection: A dark grey area. *International Journal of Refugee Law, 7*(3), 436–458.

Lischer, S. K. (2005). *Dangerous sanctuaries: Refugee camps, civil war, and the dilemmas of humanitarian aid.* Ithaca, NY: Cornell University Press.

Lung, W. C. (2019). The humanitarian assistance dilemma explained: The implications of the refugee crisis in Tanzania in 1994. *Global Change, Peace & Security, 31*(3), 323–340.

Milner, J. (2009). *Refugees, the state and the politics of Asylum in Africa.* Basingstoke: Palgrave Macmillan.

Minear, L. (2002). *The humanitarian enterprise: Dilemmas and discoveries.* Bloomfield, CT: Kumarian Press.

Mogire, E. (2006). Preventing or abetting: Refugee militarization in Tanzania. In R. Muggah (Ed.), *No refuge: The crisis of refugee militarization in Africa* (pp. 137–168). London: Zed Books.

MSF Holland. (1994). *Breaking the cycle: MSF calls for action in the Rwandese refugee camps in Tanzania and Zaire.* MSF Holland Report. Retrieved from https://www.doctorswithoutborders.org/what-we-do/news-stories/research/breaking-cycle-calls-action-rwandese-refugee-camps-tanzania-and

MSF Speaking Out. (2014a). *Genocide of Rwandan Tutsi, 1994.* Médecins Sans Frontières. (Médecins Sans Frontières Internal document). Geneva: The Médecins Sans Frontières International Movement.

MSF Speaking Out. (2014b). *Rwandan refugee camps in Zaire and Tanzania 1994-1995.* Médecins Sans Frontières. (Médecins Sans Frontières Internal document). Geneva: The Médecins Sans Frontières International Movement.

Narang, N. (2015). Assisting uncertainty: How humanitarian aid can inadvertently prolong civil war. *International Studies Quarterly, 59*(1), 184–195.

Nunn, N., & Qian, N. (2014). US food aid and civil conflict. *American Economic Review, 104*(6), 1630–1666.

OCHA. (2018). *2019 Myanmar humanitarian response plan January–December 2019.* Retrieved from https://reliefweb.int/report/myanmar/myanmar-interim-emergency-response-plan-june-december-2021-overview.

Pogge, T. (2007a). Moral priorities for International Human Rights NGOs. In D. Bell & C. Jean Marc (Eds.), *Ethics in action: The ethical challenges of international human rights nongovernmental organizations* (pp. 218–256). Cambridge: Cambridge University Press.

Pogge, T. (2007b). Assisting the global poor. In D. K. Chatterjee (Ed.), *The ethics of assistance: Morality and the distant needy* (pp. 260–289). Cambridge: Cambridge University Press.

Rieff, D. (2002). *A bed for the night: Humanitarianism in crisis.* London: Vintage.

Ruamps, C. (2022). Ethics of humanitarian action: On aid-recipients' vulnerability and humanitarian agencies' distinct obligation. *Ethics & Behavior, 32*(8), 647–657.

Shatz, A. (2002, Oct 20). *Mission impossible—humanitarianism is neutral or it is nothing.* Retrieved from http://www.msf.org/en/article/mission-impossible-humanitarianism-neutral-or-it-nothing

Slim, H. (2015). *Humanitarian ethics: A guide to the morality of aid in war and disaster.* London: Hurst Publishers.

Stockton, N. (2003). *Humanitarian values: Under siege from geopolitics.* Unpublished paper.

Swift, J., Barton, D., & Morton, J. (2002). Drought management for pastoral livelihoods–policy guidelines for Kenya. Natural Resources Institute Research, Advisory and Consultancy Projects.

Terry, F. (1999). *Reconstituting whose social order? NGOs in disrupted states.* Paper presented at the conference entitled From Civil Strife to Civil Society: Civil-Military Cooperation in Disrupted States, Canberra, Australia.

Terry, F. (2002). *Condemned to repeat? The paradox of humanitarian action.* Ithaca, NY, London: Cornell University Press.

Terry, F., & Cordaro, B. (1994). *Message from MSF France coordinator in Ngara (Tanzania) to MSF France Programme manager.* (Médecins Sans Frontières Internal document). Genève: Médecins Sans Frontières International.

The Global Humanitarian Assistance Programme of Development Initiatives. (2013). Global Humanitarian Assistance Report 2013. Retrieved from https://devinit.org/wp-content/uploads/2013/07/Global-Humanitarian-Assistance-Report-2013.pdf

The Global Humanitarian Assistance Programme of Development Initiatives. (2014). Global Humanitarian Assistance Report 2014. Retrieved from https://devinit.org/wp-content/uploads/2014/09/Global-Humanitarian-Assistance-Report-2014.pdf

The Global Humanitarian Assistance Programme of Development Initiatives. (2015). Global Humanitarian Assistance Report 2015. Retrieved from https://devinit.org/wp-content/uploads/2015/06/GHA-Report-2015_-Interactive_Online-1.pdf

Thomas, A., & Urquhart, A. (2020). *Global humanitarian assistance report 2020.* Bristol: Development Initiatives.

Timmermann, J. (2004). The individualist lottery: How people count, but not their numbers. *Analysis, 64*(2), 106–112.

Weiss, T. G. (1999). Principles, politics, and humanitarian action. *Ethics and International Affairs, 13*, 1–22.

2 The manifestation of Humanitarian Exit Dilemma

Introduction

Despite the good intentions of humanitarian organisations, humanitarian assistance and relief aid exacerbated the humanitarian crisis in Tanzania during 1994. In the case of Tanzania, humanitarian assistance relieved belligerents' burden of sustaining conflicts, created safe spaces for armed combatants, undermined local economies, bestowed legitimacy upon belligerents, and fed armed combatants. This situation hence posed the Humanitarian Exit Dilemma for humanitarian organisations. Although the shifting nature of conflicts may pose new challenges to humanitarian organisations, the fundamental Humanitarian Exit Dilemma that confronts these humanitarian organisations remains the same, regardless of agency or location of conflict (Carens, 2007; Terry, 1999).

While most scholars and aid practitioners suggest that humanitarian organisations withdraw their assistance in these contexts given the apparent negative impact of their aid, relatively little research properly identifies different kinds of ethical constraints and moral dilemmas that have long challenged humanitarian organisations. Referencing the case of late-20th-century Tanzania, this chapter contextualises the Humanitarian Exit Dilemma and systematically examines the ethical predicaments that surround it. By analysing the different manifestations of this dilemma in the refugee crisis in Tanzania in 1994, this chapter sheds light on particular kinds of moral quandaries confronting humanitarian organisations.

Tanzania has been chosen because it has presented a comparatively clear case of the Humanitarian Exit Dilemma, its corresponding ethical predicaments, and its impact on the humanitarian community. For example, it was found that the presence of armed combatants in the refugee-populated areas and the militarisation of refugee camps were

DOI: 10.4324/9781003306696-2

the most notable in Tanzania, compared to the humanitarian crisis in other countries (Milner, 2009; Mogire, 2006). It was also found that local markets had been severely affected due to the influx of aid, which drove down the prices of locally produced goods. The result was an over-dependence on aid by local authorities and victims, which further eroded an already fragile economy (Milner, 2009). Tanzania also provides an example of a man-made catastrophe that generated large numbers of refugees that the state was too weak to maintain control of due to fragility in the political and economic systems. During the Rwanda Crisis in the 1990s, approximately 700,000 Rwandan refugees entered Tanzania, which exacerbated political instability and intensified Tanzania's already fragile economic situation (Milner, 2009). Tanzania hence illustrates how the Humanitarian Exit Dilemma can manifest, as well as different ways in which ethical predicaments can occur.

This situation is reflected in most present-day conflicts. Starting from man-made disasters in the 2010s, such as the civil war fought in South Sudan in 2013, the conflict in Syria with the rise of the Islamic State in 2014, and recent humanitarian crises in Afghanistan in 2021 and in Ukraine in 2022. Take South Sudan as an example. In 2013, a political struggle between President Salva Kiir and now vice president Riek Machar resulted in violent conflict between the government forces consisting of the Dinka ethnic group and the armed opposition group 'Sudan People's Liberation Army-in Opposition' (SPLA-IO) consisting of the Nuer ethnic group. Since the outbreak of conflict, armed combatants have targeted civilians with specific ethnic backgrounds, committed rape crimes and sexual violence, destroyed property and villages, and forcefully recruited children to military force. Moreover, the violence was exacerbated by warring parties' intentional supplying of weapons to communities, leading to hundreds of thousands of civilians being killed or displaced (Aufiero & Pur, 2021; Center for Preventive Action, 2022). The violence that erupted in 2013, in short, was a result of a power struggle between the two main political leaders who manipulated ethnic divisions and grievances of the military members from the two largest ethnic groups (Dinka and Nuer) in South Sudan.

The ongoing war between Ukraine and Russia presents yet another clear example. Russian forces continued to target residential areas and bombed civilians that were located far from the frontline. Along the way, Russian troops and armies were reported to commit sexual violence against civilians, destroyed villages, and looted cities where they occupied. In addition, there have been mass detentions of civilians, forced disappearances of protestors, mock executions of people without trials, hostage-taking for political purposes, and large-scale illegal killings perpetrated by the Russian military. On 30 September 2022, Russia announced the illegal annexation of four partially occupied Ukrainian oblasts: Donetsk, Kherson, Luhansk, and Zaporizhzhia oblasts. Ever since the illegal annexation, Russia has conducted human rights violations and forced military recruitment of affected populations within these four occupied oblasts. Until recently, it has been reported that Russia is intentionally blocking and hindering humanitarian aid access in areas it occupies and controls, leaving millions of civilians in dire need of help (Besheer, 2022).

All of these conflicts share similarities with Tanzania's humanitarian crisis to a great extent. These conflicts, regardless of the timeline of the outbreak, all share in common humanitarian dilemmas: they all involve the forced recruitment of affected populations to military forces, the manipulation of international humanitarian aid for war purposes, the misappropriation of relief medical resources to shelter and benefit combatants of warring parties, and the inevitable negotiation with the armed combatants or warring parties.

In this sense, the Rwanda Crisis in 1994 in Tanzania presents an exemplary case of the types of conditions and emergency scenarios that have important implications for other countries and are indicative of how the Humanitarian Exit Dilemma can arise. While the overall situation on the African continent has evolved since the field reports and research findings were conducted, the main thrust of the findings and the implications presented remain valid.

In this chapter, I delineate how different varieties of the Humanitarian Exit Dilemma can manifest in times of conflict, using the example of the refugee crisis in Tanzania in the late 20th century. I first discuss how the Humanitarian Exit Dilemma manifests in conflicts, in general. I then use the example of the refugee crisis in Tanzania in the late 20th century as an example to show how the Humanitarian Exit Dilemma induces different types of ethical predicaments for humanitarian organisations. I contend that the Humanitarian Exit Dilemma often manifests in conflicts in five crucial ways. Different kinds of ethical predicaments arise accordingly, depending on how the Humanitarian Exit Dilemma manifests in conflicts. I elaborate on this point in the following section.

Before proceeding, it is important to note that this book is a work of moral theory and political philosophy. Hence, no interviews were involved, and no field research was conducted. Tanzania and some other countries are referred to with the use of secondary resources as illuminating cases to help facilitate exposition and underpin arguments. This chapter uses a range of primary documents from Médecins Sans Frontières (MSF) and other humanitarian organisations.

Tanzania from 1960 to 1994

After gaining independence in the 1960s, Tanzania hosted tens of thousands of refugees fleeing national liberation movements and post-colonial conflicts. Back then, Tanzania was regarded as one of the most hospitable asylum-granting countries in Africa (Milner, 2009). However, such an open-door policy of asylum-granting changed in the 1990s. This was due in large part to the magnitude of refugee population inflows since the 1960s, the economic breakdown in Tanzania in the 1980s, the shifting of Tanzanian authorities' political ideology in the 1990s, the security concerns provoked by refugees in Tanzania after the Rwandan Crisis in 1994, and the overall lack of support from the international community to help deal with this crisis (Milner, 2009).

From the 1960s to the 1970s, motivated by former President Julius Kambarage Nyerere's economic strategy, an open asylum policy was implemented in Tanzania. Nyerere regarded the presence of refugees as advantageous because they helped attract support from international donors. Nyerere intended to accommodate as many refugees as possible to attract funds to accelerate Tanzania's economic development (Milner, 2009). Therefore, the settlement of refugees in Tanzania was "guided by the concepts of permanence and productivity, stemming...from the principles on which the President...hoped to develop his country" (Yéfime, 1988, p.13). In fact, Nyerere's strategy was to use refugees as a tool purely for economic matters (Yéfime, 1988).

In addition to his economic development strategy, Nyerere provided support to liberation movements in other African countries during this period in following his 'pan-Africanism' political ideology (Milner, 2009). Tanzania adopted "a strategy of encouraging and supporting armed struggles by the African populations" (Nnoli, 1978, p.80). As a result of this ideology, Tanzania harboured rebel movements that allowed armed combatants to recruit refugees as their soldiers, to receive contributions from refugees, and to use refugee camps to launch insurgencies (Mogire, 2006). For instance, Tanzania was charged with exacerbating the civil war in Burundi by providing military training for rebel groups at its border and supporting rebel groups' liberation movements in the 1970s.

The intensity of conflict between Tanzania and its neighbouring countries since the 1960s, the collapse of its domestic economies in the 1980s, and the Rwanda Crisis in the 1990s would eventually lead to Tanzanian authorities being labelled as a failed state.

The refugee crisis in Tanzania in 1994

From Rwandan Independence in 1962 to April 1994, around 50,000 Tutsi Rwandese refugees fled to Tanzania (Vassall-Adams, 1994). Most of them were initially settled in a camp at Muyenzi in the Ngara district and later at a camp at Mwesi (Vassall-Adams, 1994). According to Human Rights Watch (HRW), in the space of 100 days between April and July 1994, at least half a million Tutsis were killed, amounting to "three quarters of the Tutsi population of Rwanda" (Des Forges, 1999, p.12). Overall, an estimated 800,000 Rwandans died in Rwanda (Des Forges, 1999). Following the murders of the former Rwandan President Juvénal Habyarimana and former Burundian President Cyprien Ntaryamira on Ntaryamira 6 April 1994, there was an increased influx of refugees to Tanzania.

The Tanzanian government hosted approximately "255,000 refugees in Benaco camp, 98,000 in Lumasi and 30,000 in Musuhura" in response to the unprecedented flow of refugees (MSF Holland, 1994, p.4). Despite its reputation as one of the most welcoming asylum countries, Tanzania was accused of encouraging and supporting rebel groups in their armed movements. As noted earlier, Tanzanian authorities were found to harbour rebel movements against Burundi. In a similar vein, during the Rwanda Crisis in the 1990s, it was found that Forces Armées Rwandaises (FAR) were present in the Tanzanian camps, where military structures existed, and stocks of arms and training activities were found (MSF Speaking Out, 2014a, 2014b).

Shocked by the unprecedented scale of people in need affected by the Rwanda Crisis, many humanitarian organisations established their presence as a response. International humanitarian organisations such as the International Committee of the Red Cross (ICRC), Médecins Sans Frontières (MSF), and Oxfam (the UK and Ireland) launched numerous humanitarian projects throughout the Great Lakes region of Africa during the crisis. While Oxfam (the UK and Ireland) launched one of the largest emergency operations in response to this disaster, MSF provided ample relief aid and medical resources to the affected population (MSF Speaking Out, 2014a, 2014b; Vassall-Adams, 1994). According to Guy Vassall-Adams, most of the operations were performed by "ICRC (food supplies), MSF (health care), Oxfam (water supplies), and CARE (non-food items)" (1994, p.49).

However, humanitarian assistance and relief aid provided by humanitarian organisations during this crisis exacerbated the conflict and intensified the ongoing suffering, despite their good intentions. This situation posed the typical Humanitarian Exit Dilemma for humanitarian organisations: seeing that their humanitarian efforts can cause more harm overall, humanitarian organisations often have to decide whether to withdraw their assistance. In the case of Tanzania, the Humanitarian Exit Dilemma manifests itself in five main ways in the context of conflict: humanitarian assistance relieved armed combatants' burden of sustaining conflicts, created safe spaces for armed combatants, undermined local coping strategies, bestowed legitimacy upon armed combatants, and fed armed combatants. This is discussed further below.

Overall, the example of Tanzania shows three important facts. First, it shows that humanitarian organisations, in effect, profess differing fundamental purposes, humanitarian operational principles, and organisational mandates when carrying out humanitarian operations. Second, it reflects that, due to such differences, humanitarian organisations lack a clear consensus regarding which action is the right one to take and also which right action to prioritise in the face of the Humanitarian Exit Dilemma. Finally, it clearly depicts the kind of Humanitarian Exit Dilemma and ethical predicaments facing humanitarian organisations (which is shown in the subsequent discussion).

Before proceeding, it is important to note that this book focuses on humanitarian organisations that concentrate on relief aid and humanitarian assistance provision in fragile and extreme emergency settings, such as ICRC and MSF. Therefore, bilateral, and multilateral, aid that state actors, governments, or governmental organisations provide is not taken into account. The humanitarian organisations stated above may profess different mandates: some may profess a charitable duty to assist the most vulnerable, whereas others may base their action on the basic human rights of individuals by virtue of humanity. Nevertheless, they all have certain important humanitarian features in common: the humanitarian organisations noted above all have the common objective of alleviating the affected population's suffering and prioritising the concern for humanity over other considerations (Carens, 2007).

Most importantly, these humanitarian organisations all face the Humanitarian Exit Dilemma that agencies working exclusively on development projects would not face. This is because humanitarian organisations such as MSF often perform humanitarian operations in the context of violence, insecurity, and extreme emergency in contrast to development agencies (Barnett, 2011).

Humanitarian organisations' frequent struggles with the Humanitarian Exit Dilemma are also due in large part to their commitment to humanitarian guiding principles, such as neutrality and impartiality, which is not the case for agencies working in development projects (Abu-Sada, 2012; Fast, 2014; Hilhorst, 2002).

Five Humanitarian Exit Dilemma manifestations

The Humanitarian Exit Dilemma can arise in five crucial ways, and each way, respectively, poses an ethical predicament for humanitarian organisations.

Reducing armed combatants' costs

Humanitarian assistance can relieve armed combatants' burden of sustaining costly conflicts by providing material resources they need to finance their attacks and support their insurgencies. Humanitarian assistance, therefore, can be used as an instrument for armed combatants to exploit and benefit from. Armed combatants often misappropriate material and food resources that are meant to help the affected population, regardless of humanitarian organisations' unwillingness. As a result, relief aid is found to enable armed combatants to launch less costly attacks.

For instance, research on Rwandan refugee camps in Tanzania demonstrates that those who were "suspected of participating in the genocide... were officially assigned to draw up lists of beneficiaries and to organise distributions of food aid provided by the World Food Programme (WFP), much of which they misappropriated" (MSF Speaking Out, 2014b, p.12). Sarah Lischer's findings also suggest that armed combatants benefitted from exaggerating the number of refugees present, in addition to misappropriating vast quantities of relief aid and humanitarian resources to sustain costly conflicts (Lischer, 2005). Furthermore, according to Lischer and James Milner, armed combatants often hid their families in the camps in order to relieve their demands of food and goods (Milner, 2009). For example, it was found that armed combatants settled their family members in the refugee camp "as a destination for rest and relaxation, and as a source for supplies" (Milner, 2009, p.152). Finally, John Prendergast points out that 'selling or trading diverted commodities' was "a principal method of obtaining weapons for armed combatants in conflicts" (Prendergast & Bennett, 1996, p.22). Humanitarian assistance, to that extent, relieved armed combatants' burdens to sustain costly conflicts. While humanitarian assistance can provide incentives for conflicts by relieving armed combatants' burdens to feed their family members, it also incentivises conflict by intensifying existing suffering. According to a report conducted in 1994 by MSF, it was evident at that time that the "distribution of humanitarian relief is being controlled and aid is often diverted by community leaders, many of whom themselves are suspected of having been involved in the genocide", which resulted in the prolongation of the Rwandan conflict (MSF Holland, 1994).[1] This further supports the claim that humanitarian assistance has, in effect, been relieving the burden of armed combatants. Knowing that their humanitarian assistance could be and had been misused or used against those it was supposed to support, humanitarian organisations such as MSF-France decided to withdraw their support in the face of the obvious negative impact of their assistance (MSF Speaking Out, 2014a, 2014b).

Therefore, the corresponding ethical predicament is this: should humanitarian organisations stay and remain engaged with the current affected population but risk providing incentives for conflicts?

Providing safe spaces for armed combatants

The Humanitarian Exit Dilemma can also arise when humanitarian organisations create safe spaces for armed combatants, leading to the forced recruitment of refugees, the militarisation of refugee camps, and human rights violations in refugee-populated areas. Relief aid and humanitarian resources delivered to refugee camps often provide cover for armed combatants and further facilitate the process of the militarisation of refugee camps. In addition, humanitarian assistance and the aid provided also enable armed combatants to conduct human rights violations (MSF Holland, 1994; MSF Speaking Out, 2014a, 2014b).

For example, Bernard Pécoul, the MSF-France Executive Director at the time, argued that "the rehabilitation of the torturers under cover of international humanitarian aid" was found everywhere in the Rwandan refugee camp in Benaco in Tanzania, which made the camp "a humanitarian façade" (MSF Speaking Out, 2014a, p.51). The control of the Benaco camp by the armed combatants responsible for genocide made it, as termed by Pécoul, a 'Hutu stronghold' (MSF Speaking Out, 2014a, p.51). Moreover, the presence of armed combatants in the camps in Tanzania severely threatened the lives of refugees in these camps. Human rights violations were also identified in refugee settlements. For instance, Nicolas de Torrente, MSF-France's administrator in Tanzania between 1993 and 1994, found that humanitarian assistance to refugee camps not only provided a perfect cover for armed combatants to hide but also enabled them to conduct killings more easily (MSF Speaking Out, 2014a, 2014b). Other human rights violations such as forced recruitment were also evident at that time. According to MSF-USA, "military training of refugees is openly conducted near the camps", and "killings and intimidation in the camps happen on a daily basis", where "refugees in the camps are not free to choose whether to return or not" (MSF Speaking Out, 2014b, p.72). In a similar vein, Mogire found that armed combatants in Tanzania not only recruited and trained refugees but also used refugee camps to conduct cross-border insurgencies (Mogire, 2006). According to Integrated Regional Information Networks (IRIN), there was strong evidence indicating that forced recruitment and forced taxation were taking place inside refugee camps in Tanzania (Mogire, 2006). Given that some humanitarian organisations, such as MSF-France, were uncertain about the identities of armed combatants that hid and rested in the camp, they were incapable of distinguishing between armed combatants and genuine refugees (MSF Speaking Out, 2014a, 2014b).

Another example was found in some of MSF's minutes recorded in 1994. According to the minutes, Hutu rebel groups' armed movements were "well organised with lists" and local leaders hiding in the camps had "total control of the population", which made the camp "become a haven for the FAR, shielded by the civilian population" (MSF Speaking Out, 2014b, p.14). Furthermore, it was evident that "the figures stating number of refugees in the camp has been overestimated" by armed combatants in order to attract more influx of aid for their own use (MSF Speaking Out, 2014b, p.14). According to the data retrieved from the report, *MSF calls for action in the Rwandese refugee camps in Tanzania and Zaire*, there is evidence that FAR were present in the Tanzanian camps, where military structures existed, and stocks of arms and training activities were found. Specifically, in 'the former Rwandese army' section of MSF Holland's report, it states that "the FAR is present in the camps in Zaire, Mugunga near Goma and Chimanga near Bukavu and in the Tanzanian camps. They live with their families among the refugees. A military structure continues to exist, and stocks of arms and training activities have been reported. The market in Mugunga camp is extremely well-supplied and bags of relief goods are openly being traded" (MSF Holland, 1994, p.3). Terry also supports this finding by stating that armed combatants used protected camps and aid to enclave safe zones to rest and recruit combatants (2002).

Thus, the Humanitarian Exit Dilemma creates protected safe spaces for armed combatants. Furthermore, Narang finds that this phenomenon is ongoing, with humanitarian assistance still being misused by armed combatants to hide, recruit more armed combatants, and launch further attacks (Narang, 2015). These findings further support the argument that although humanitarian assistance provides help to refugees in camps, it can also become a cover, providing protected safe spaces for armed combatants. When humanitarian assistance creates protected safe spaces for armed combatants, human rights violations can arise. To conclude, humanitarian organisations often have no choice but to provide humanitarian assistance not only to the genuine refugees but also to the armed combatants in camps. By creating safe spaces and covers for combatants, humanitarian organisations are often forced to facilitate and therefore condone, obvious human rights violations in these refugee camps and settlements.

The corresponding ethical predicament facing humanitarian organisations then is this: should humanitarian organisations stay and remain engaged with the current affected population but risk encouraging human rights violations?

Undermining local economies

The Humanitarian Exit Dilemma may also arise when humanitarian assistance undermines local coping strategies to deal with crises. In times of conflict, humanitarian assistance can strengthen the existing power relations of the camp and further support wartime economies. This phenomenon often erodes local capacities to deal with emergencies and further collapses local economies. In addition to undermining local coping strategies and paralysing local economies, humanitarian assistance can also stunt development, corrupt social structures, weaken peacetime productivity, and exacerbate market imbalances (Anderson, 1998, 1999; Stockton, 2003). In these situations, the affected population is often forced to continue to rely on relief aid for survival. This has contributed to their dependence on aid significantly. As Mary Anderson notes in her findings, the influx of humanitarian resources often reinforces individuals' interests in maintaining wartime economies, especially when conflicts have severely disrupted local economies where almost no local capacities exist (1999).

Humanitarian assistance can also encourage wartime economies. It was found that "the Hutu government lost the war but maintained control of the population and economic resources" through humanitarian organisations and humanitarian assistance (MSF Speaking Out, 2014b, p.28). Withdrawing aid was necessary because it was evident that the Hutu government's "entire economic survival is ... based on this bluff and trafficking of aid" (MSF Speaking Out, 2014b, p.28).

In addition to supporting wartime economies, humanitarian assistance also reinforced the existing power structures in camps, which resulted in refugees' further dependence on relief aid (MSF Speaking Out, 2014b). This phenomenon is particularly evident when armed combatants misappropriate humanitarian resources and resell relief aid to refugees. For example, in the Ngara refugee camp in Tanzania, it was found that "many water points are ... under the control of a man known to UNHCR who sells the water to the refugees" (Terry & Cordaro, 1994, p.1). It was also found that armed combatants were able to set up a taxation system on food, which combatant leaders profited from because of the power they had gained in the camp (Terry & Cordaro, 1994). This situation can make refugees in camps even more vulnerable and more in need of aid.

By supporting wartime economies and strengthening the existing power imbalance in camps, humanitarian assistance can further contribute to the already vulnerable refugees' dependency on aid. It was evident that the armed combatants of the former Rwandan government were able to "consolidate their power over the 300,000 Rwandans" only because they used "the daily food distributions" as a bargain (MSF Speaking Out, 2014b, p.34). Furthermore, refugees were made even more dependent on relief aid in situations where local economies were disrupted, and humanitarian resources were under the control of armed combatants (MSF Speaking Out, 2014b). Armed combatants had received more aid by making up the number of refugees, and this had successfully persuaded refugees to remain in camps (MSF Speaking Out, 2014b). By controlling the aid, armed combatants had also successfully kept refugees under their control: refugees were found to remain in the camp not only because local economies were too weak to sustain their basic livelihood, but also because armed combatants had control over aid resources. This demonstrates that humanitarian assistance can make refugees even more vulnerable and more dependent on aid in the long run. After all, in situations where humanitarian assistance undermines local capacities, reinforces wartime economies, and strengthens the existing power imbalance, refugees are more inclined to depend on aid and are often made more vulnerable.

The corresponding ethical predicament is this: should humanitarian organisations stay and remain engaged with the current affected population but risk undermining local economies?

Bestowing legitimacy upon armed combatants

The Humanitarian Exit Dilemma can also arise when humanitarian assistance legitimises armed combatants' unjust regimes. Humanitarian organisations are often forced to negotiate with armed combatants who are in control of refugee camps to get access to the affected population. This includes agreeing to hire armed combatants as safeguards and paying taxes to armed combatants. To that extent, humanitarian organisations have contributed to armed combatants' perceived legitimacy. Through their collaboration and cooperation with the armed combatants, humanitarian organisations bestow legitimacy. Armed combatants often perceive their regimes as legitimate and lawful, due in large part to humanitarian organisations' cooperation and collaboration with them (Anderson, 1999). They hence come to expect that "external aid agencies will comply with the rules and restrictions they impose in their area of command" (Anderson, 1999, p.50).

The findings of several reports, including those by MSF-USA and MSF-France, also support the claim that armed combatants often establish their legitimacy to rule over refugee populations through collaborating and cooperating with humanitarian organisations in the field (MSF Speaking Out, 2014b; Terry & Cordaro, 2004). For instance, by hiring "a group of 300 Rwandans to oversee security during registration and food distributions and to patrol in the camps", who appeared to be complicitous with the armed combatants, United Nations High Commissioner for Refugees (UNHCR) had strengthened armed combatants' authority to control the camps and legitimised armed combatants' rule over refugee populations (MSF Speaking Out, 2014b, p.13).

Another example can be found in MSF-USA's press release in 1994. The press release suggested that their collaboration with armed combatants strengthened and legitimised "the power of leaders of a regime which organized and perpetrated a genocide", which left them no choice but to withdraw their assistance from Rwandan refugee camps in Tanzania (MSF Speaking Out, 2014b, p.72). According to the press release, armed combatants were appointed as "the official and paid mediators between the aid agencies and the refugees", who were in charge of selecting 'the candidates for the refugee police force or guardians' in refugee camps in Tanzania (MSF Speaking

Out, 2014b, p.72). To that extent, humanitarian organisations helped institutionalise armed combatants' power and legitimacy in camps, and bestowed legitimacy upon them by granting them the right to select candidates in camps and rule over refugees. Knowing that they had legitimised armed combatants' unjust regime, MSF-USA decided to withdraw their assistance in order to avoid being complicit in armed combatants' wrongdoing (MSF Speaking Out, 2014b).

Furthermore, MSF-France's report suggested that "it is very clear that humanitarian aid to the Rwandan refugees helps maintain the power of the leaders" because "all NGOs and UN agencies working in the Tanzania camps operate through a structure which reinforces the control of the leaders" (Terry & Cordaro, 2004). This situation was found to further empower "the leaders... to ensure compliance [with] this system of taxation" (Terry & Cordaro, 2004, p.1). Hence, field reports of MSF-France and MSF-USA support the claim that humanitarian organisations can legitimise the armed combatants' oppressive regime by collaborating and cooperating with them.

The corresponding ethical predicament that arises is this: should humanitarian organisations stay and remain engaged with the current affected population but risk bestowing legitimacy upon armed combatants?

Feeding armed combatants

Finally, humanitarian assistance can directly feed armed combatants' basic needs through humanitarian organisations' commitment to the traditional humanitarian operational principles of impartiality and neutrality. This manifestation of the Humanitarian Exit Dilemma differs from the first manifestation of the dilemma (i.e., the Humanitarian Exit Dilemma arising in situations where humanitarian assistance relieves armed combatants' cost). The latter involves the misappropriation of resources, while the former involves feeding all needy people impartially or neutrally.

The principles of impartiality and neutrality are two of the core principles of humanitarian action. The former focuses on providing aid according to need and without discrimination; the latter focuses on the importance of not taking sides in conflicts (Abu-Sada, 2012; Barnett, 2011; ECHO & ODI, 1998; Fast, 2014; Harroff-Tavel, 1989; Hoffman & Weiss, 2006; Minear & Weiss, 1993). The traditional operational principle of impartiality is regarded by many as one of the fundamental principles of humanitarian action, given that it guarantees an approach that is about assisting needy people in acute danger without discrimination (von Pilar, 1999). Impartiality is a "true reflection of ... humanity" (von Pilar, 1999, p.3). Bearing this in mind, humanitarian organisations often deliver humanitarian action and emergency assistance based on the operational principle of impartiality. However, this sometimes involves assisting armed combatants. This is because the operational principles of impartiality demand humanitarian organisations assist every needy person "irrespective of their being part of any social, political, ethnic or another group" (von Pilar, 1999, p.3). Although a commitment to impartiality can help humanitarian organisations reflect their belief in humanity, many view it as outdated. This is because the principle of impartiality often benefits not only the genuine refugees but also the obvious wrongdoers (i.e., armed combatants, rebel groups, belligerents, etc.).

Although humanitarian organisations working in Tanzania could tell that the refugees were organised and there was a structure existing in the camp, they nevertheless continued to provide medical support to them, based on their operational principle of impartiality (MSF Speaking Out, 2014b). As a result, "huge quantities of food were distributed which the leaders resold. The same trucks that brought food in went back out again full" (MSF Speaking Out, 2014b, p.13). MSF's medical mandate in aiding needy people impartially thus led to an unwanted outcome: tens of thousands of murderers received aid. They were thereby enabled to conduct more killings as a result of this aid.

Another example of humanitarian assistance feeding armed combatants because of humanitarian organisations' commitments to impartiality can be found in the Tanzanian Red Cross report. The report clearly stated that doctors working in camps had helped feed armed combatants and further enabled them to do more harm because they believed in the principle of impartiality. Hervé Isambert, who worked for the Tanzanian Red Cross, for instance, saw the wounded murderers of Tutsi "burst into the Rwandan hospital where he was working" and left the camp upon recovery (MSF Speaking Out, 2014b, p.14). Even though he knew that the patients he treated were killers and murderers, Isambert insisted that the principle of impartiality is of utmost importance since it is "everything that humanitarianism stands for" (MSF Speaking Out, 2014b, p.14). Also, Christine Pliche, a nurse working in the hospital in Rwanda, re-asserted her commitment to the traditional principle of impartiality: "I work in medicine and I have my professional code of ethics and because of this, 'I close my eyes and I treat people'" (MSF Speaking Out, 2014b, p.14).

Furthermore, the spokesman of UNHCR at that time, Philippe Lamair, reiterates humanitarian organisations' mandate of impartiality and neutrality in delivering humanitarian assistance by arguing that "qualms are a personal issue" that cannot be used to deny people's right to care (MSF Speaking Out, 2014b, p.14). A manager from CARE even goes so far as to defend its commitment to traditional humanitarian operational principles of impartiality and neutrality by contending that, as humanitarian organisations, they cannot refuse to aid armed combatants just because they are the repressors (MSF Speaking Out, 2014b).

Finally, in Hanna Nolan's memo from the Department of Humanitarian Affairs of MSF Holland, MSF Holland's head office defended and justified its position of staying in camps (1994). According to Nolan's memo, MSF Holland's head office was struggling to decide whether to "continue to give humanitarian aid to people", especially to "whom it is said that while receiving the good care of the aid agencies they are preparing themselves for a return to Rwanda to continue their murderous practices" (MSF Speaking Out, 2014b, p.24). MSF Belgium staff who worked in the Benaco camp in Tanzania were found to have felt uneasy about aiding: "individuals in the Benaco camp ... suspected of having participated in acts of genocide or other violations of human rights in Rwanda" (MSF Speaking Out, 2014b, p.24). However, MSF Holland's head office restated its commitment to the principle of impartiality: "MSF's charter demands us to give humanitarian aid indiscriminately. We should continue our activities in the camp" because humanitarian organisations "are not judges who would have the evidence to decide who is guilty of such a crime". After all, "choosing to whom to give or not give aid would be impossible" (MSF Speaking Out, 2014b, p.24).

As Wouter Kok, MSF Holland's coordinator in Tanzania at the time, puts it, we "can have judgements but we cannot use our aid to punish the bad guys", given that it is "not the role of a medical organisation"; "it is up to a judge to decide who is to be punished" (MSF Speaking Out, 2014b, p.67). Kok furthers this statement by arguing that "we can advocate, and we can highlight a problem, but we should not use our relief—be it health care, be it food or be it water—to distinguish between good and bad" (MSF Speaking Out, 2014b, p.67). Having a strong commitment to the mandate of impartiality, humanitarian organisations often feel obliged to fulfil this commitment, even if it means that their aid enables the 'bad guys' to launch further attacks and cause more suffering.

While the principle of impartiality can enable wrongdoers to take advantage of aid resources, the principle of neutrality can, furthermore, encourage repressors to continue to cause harm. The main difference between these two principles of humanitarian action lies in that the former can benefit wrongdoers by aiding indiscriminately, whereas the latter can encourage repressors to continue causing harm by making no judgements and staying silent. By staying neutral, making no judgements, and remaining silent on repressors' mass abuse of refugees, the principle of neutrality can encourage repressors to continue to cause harm. By committing to traditional operational principles of impartiality and neutrality, humanitarian organisations are often accused of "being blind to injustice" and "acting indiscriminately as quartermaster to the forces of … evil" (Stockton, 2003, p.6). This is mainly because humanitarian assistance often feeds armed combatants and enables them to cause more harm. Hence, humanitarian organisations and the assistance they provide often make the overall situation even more problematic, rather than alleviating genuine refugees' suffering.

This specific type of ethical predicament differs from the other four ethical predicaments discussed above. Instead of choosing between continuing their humanitarian operations and minimising the negative impacts of aid, humanitarian organisations are forced to choose between upholding principles of impartiality and neutrality and adopting different but equally important humanitarian operational principles to avoid harm.

Overall ethical predicaments evaluated

As shown above, humanitarian assistance and the relief aid provided can generate difficult ethical predicaments and have profound negative impacts on the affected population in conflict-affected settings. Knowing that aid can be counter-productive in humanitarian crises, numerous theorists and aid practitioners have argued that humanitarian assistance should either be withdrawn or reallocated. This is based on the belief that, overall, humanitarian assistance has generated a more negative rather than positive impact on the affected population, and that aid should be delivered in a more cost-effective way that can reduce harm and preserve more lives (Barber, 1997; Glennie, 2010; Lischer, 2005; Nunn & Qian, 2012; Pogge, 2007a, 2007b; Terry, 2002).

Granted that humanitarian assistance may have a profound negative impact, humanitarian organisations' efforts are still typically *humanitarian*—they operate missions (if not always solely) for *reasons of humanity*. It follows that simply focusing on the results of projects, such as the overall efficacy of humanitarian operations and the number of lives helped, is inadequate. Calculating all possible negative impacts of humanitarian assistance, after all, does not help humanitarian organisations navigate their decisions when confronted with the Humanitarian Exit Dilemma and its corresponding ethical predicaments. Starting with what can be measured, such as quantifiable indicators, rather than what should be measured can lead to meaningless evaluations of humanitarian operations (Autesserre, 2014).

Most of the existing literature on humanitarian assistance mainly considers the negative impact of humanitarian assistance and thus views the continuation of assistance as causing more harm. This trend in current humanitarian discourse, therefore, unsurprisingly, is dominated by arguments on aid effectiveness and aid efficiency, in light of the view that humanitarian organisations should promote the best outcome. This requires humanitarian organisations to maximise the utility of relief aid and to withdraw their assistance to refugees if necessary (Barber, 1997; Barnett, 2011; Boyd, 1995; De Waal, 1997; Hoffman & Weiss, 2006; Lischer, 2005; Pogge, 2007a, 2007b; Terry, 1999; Weiss, 1999; Weiss & Collins, 2000). This phenomenon seems to have developed due to the popularity of a simple account of consequentialism for resolving the Humanitarian Exit Dilemma.

Humanitarian organisations often emphatically adopt a simple account of consequentialism to calculate costs and benefits when facing the Humanitarian Exit Dilemma (Gross, 2009). The scarcity of resources and the limitation of time further reinforce humanitarian organisations' belief that maximising the utility of aid and resources in a cost-effective way appears to be the most reasonable way to approach the Humanitarian Exit Dilemma. Given the fact that conflicts create mass-casualty triage, where the scarcity of resources and the limitation of time make it impossible to save all lives, humanitarian organisations often follow a utilitarian calculation, favouring the welfare of the larger number of people over that of the smaller number of people (Gross, 2009).

There is no doubt that overall consequences matter and that the simple account of consequentialism stated above could be a way to resolve the Humanitarian Exit Dilemma. Indeed, at first glance, the simple account of consequentialism appears to be intuitively attractive, given that it rightly appeals to one's intuition that it is important to maximise harm-reduction. However, humanitarian organisations often have different beliefs about crisis response, holding different expectations of humanitarian assistance, subscribing to varying principles of humanitarian action, and endorsing different ethical norms. It follows that different humanitarian organisations may face different moral dilemmas when delivering relief aid in conflicts. Depending on their operational principles and organisational structures, they may face volitional moral dilemmas, cognitive moral dilemmas, or social moral dilemmas (Dubois, 2008).

For instance, volitional moral dilemmas pose predicaments to humanitarian organisations when they know the right course of action but are unsure whether they can perform the action successfully. However, cognitive moral dilemmas are dilemmas in which humanitarian organisations are unsure which action is best to take. Different to both volitional moral dilemmas and cognitive moral dilemmas, social moral dilemmas are dilemmas occurring in cases where different humanitarian organisations disagree on the right course of action (Dubois, 2008). Therefore, it is of great importance to lay out the five ethical quandaries facing humanitarian organisations when delivering relief aid in conflicts.

Conclusion

This chapter used the example of Tanzania to show how the Humanitarian Exit Dilemma arises, different ways the Humanitarian Exit Dilemma can manifest itself in conflicts, and its specific corresponding ethical predicaments. It first showed that the Humanitarian Exit Dilemma can manifest itself in conflicts when humanitarian assistance relieves armed combatants' burden of sustaining costly conflicts, creates protected spaces for armed combatants, undermines local coping strategies, bestows legitimacy upon armed combatants, and directly feeds armed combatants. It then identified five distinct ethical predicaments that link humanitarian assistance to the Humanitarian Exit Dilemma in conflicts. These are the ethical predicaments of providing incentives for conflicts, allowing human rights violations, creating refugees' dependency on aid, being complicit in armed combatants' wrongdoings, and feeding unjust combatants.

Finally, it sheds light on five core moral quandaries humanitarian organisations and aid agencies need to address in conflicts whether to stay and remain engaged with the most vulnerable populations but provide an incentive for conflicts, set up refugee camps for the affected population but risk allowing human rights violations, provide presumptively important goods to refugees but risk creating their dependency on aid, collaborate with armed combatants but risk being complicit in their wrongdoing, and provide aid indiscriminately but risk enabling armed combatants to do more harm. These moral quandaries, altogether, pose an overall dilemmatic question to humanitarian organisations: should humanitarian organisations stay and remain engaged with *some refugees*, or should humanitarian organisations leave and reallocate the aid to other places where aid has fewer negative impacts (and hence *more people can benefit*)?

To properly answer this question, there is a need for further investigation of different moral issues underlying the ethical constraints embedded in the Humanitarian Exit Dilemma and the entailed ethical predicaments. Although there are good reasons to think that relief aid exacerbates conflicts and generates more harm in the long run, and should thus be withdrawn and reallocated, humanitarian organisations may want to stay stationed in areas of need for other weighty moral reasons, such as the moral significance of humanitarian assistance's non-instrumental values. These values will be discussed and elaborated on in depth in the following three chapters.

The Humanitarian Exit Dilemma and its corresponding ethical predicaments associated with humanitarian assistance in Tanzania remain highly relevant to the existing literature on humanitarian assistance. Although the shifting nature of conflicts may pose new challenges to humanitarian organisations, the fundamental Humanitarian Exit Dilemma that confronts humanitarian organisations is essentially the same as in the past. This is because the decisions humanitarian organisations need to make regarding aid allocation (i.e., withdrawing, reallocating, or staying) when they encounter the Humanitarian Exit Dilemma in conflicts, as outlined in this chapter, remain the same.

The Humanitarian Exit Dilemma and the ethical predicaments it entails can be viewed as a dilemma between non-instrumental values and the overall consequences. Humanitarian organisations need to consider morally weighty non-instrumental values in order to justify the decisions made when confronted with the Humanitarian Exit Dilemma. These values can provide justifications for humanitarian organisations' continued assistance, over the need to prevent greater harm and preserve more lives at times. To shed light on this matter, Chapters 3, 4, and 5 show how certain non-instrumental values, such as special relationships, distinct dependence, and reasonable expectations, can be given precedence over overall consequences sometimes. Chapter 6, on this basis, seeks to develop more general guidelines for weighing the competing values at stake.

Note

1 Note that this specific Humanitarian Exit Dilemma, namely reducing armed combatants' costs, also happened in Zaire (the former DR Congo).

References

Abu-Sada, C. (2012). *In the eyes of others: How people in crises perceive humanitarian aid.* New York: Médecins Sans Frontières-USA (MSF-USA).

Anderson, M. B. (1998). You save my life today, but for what tomorrow? In J. Moore (Ed.), *Hard choice: Moral dilemmas in humanitarian intervention.* Lanham, MD: Rowman & Littlefield.

Anderson, M. B. (1999). *Do no harm: How aid can support peace—Or war.* London: Lynne Rienner Publishers.

Aufiero, P. & Pur, N. T. (2021, July 9). *South Sudan at a crossroads: Challenges and hopes 10 years after independence.* Human Rights Watch (HRW). Retrieved from https://www.hrw.org/news/2021/07/09/south-sudan-crossroads

Autesserre, S. (2014). *Peaceland conflict: Resolution and the everyday politics of international intervention.* Cambridge: Cambridge University Press.

Barber, B. (1997). Feeding refugees, or war? The dilemma of humanitarian aid. *Foreign Affairs, 76*(4), 8–14.

Barnett, M. (2011). *The empire of humanity: A history of humanitarianism.* Ithaca, NY: Cornell University Press.

Besheer, M. (2022). *Millions of Ukrainians beyond reach, as Russia blocks UN aid access in areas it controls.* Retrieved from https://www.voanews.com/a/millions-of-ukrainians-beyond-reach-as-russia-blocks-un-aid-access-in-areas-it-controls/6798436.html

Boyd, C. (1995). Making peace with the guilty. *Foreign Affairs, 74*(5), 22–38.

Carens, J. (2007). The problem of doing good in a world that isn't: Reflections on the ethical challenges facing INGOs. In D. Bell & J. Coicaud (Eds.), *Ethics in action* (pp. 257–272). Cambridge: Cambridge University Press.

Center for Preventive Action. (2022). *Civil war in South Sudan.* Retrieved from https://www.cfr.org/glo bal-conflict-tracker/conflict/civil-war-south-sudan

De Waal, A. (1997). *Famine crimes: Politics and the disaster relief industry in Africa.* Oxford: James Currey.

Des Forges, A. (1999). *Leave none to tell the story: Genocide in Rwanda.* Human Rights Watch.

DuBois, J. M. (2008). Ethics in mental health research: Principles, guidance, cases. New York: Oxford University Press.

ECHO & ODI. (1998). Report of: *ECHO/ ODI conference on principled aid in an unprincipled world: Relief, war and humanitarian principles.* London.

Fast, L. (2014). *Aid in danger: The perils and promise of humanitarianism.* Philadelphia: University of Pennsylvania Press.

Glennie, J. (2010). More aid is not the answer. *The Journal of Contemporary World Affairs, 109*(727), 205.

Gross, M. (2009). *Moral dilemmas of modern war: Torture, assassination, and blackmail in an age of asymmetric conflict.* Cambridge: Cambridge University Press. https://doi.org/10.1017/CBO9780511811562

Harroff-Tavel, M. (1989). Neutrality and impartiality—The importance of these principles for the International Red Cross and Red Crescent Movement and the difficulties involved in applying them. *International Review of the Red Cross, 29*(273), 536–552.

Hilhorst, D. (2002). Being good at doing good? Quality and accountability of humanitarian NGOs. *Disasters, 26*(3), 193–212.

Hoffman, P., & Weiss, T. G. (2006). *Sword & salve: Confronting new wars and humanitarian crises.* Lanham, MD: Rowman & Littlefield.

Lischer, S. K. (2005). Dangerous sanctuaries: Refugee camps, civil war, and the dilemmas of humanitarian aid. *Cornell Studies in Security Affairs, 204.*

Milner, J. (2009). *Refugees, the state and the politics of Asylum in Africa.* Basingstoke: Palgrave Macmillan.

Minear, L., & Weiss, T. (1993). *Humanitarian action in times of war: A handbook for practitioners.* London: Lynne Rienner.

Mogire, E. (2006). Preventing or abetting: Refugee militarization in Tanzania. In R. Muggah (Ed.), *No refuge: The crisis of refugee militarization in Africa* (pp. 137–168). London: Zed Books.

MSF Holland. (1994). *Breaking the cycle: MSF calls for action in the Rwandese refugee camps in Tanzania and Zaire.* MSF Holland Report. Retrieved from https://www.doctorswithoutborders.org/what-we-do/news-stories/research/breaking-cycle-calls-action-rwandese-refugee-camps-tanzania-and

MSF Speaking Out. (2014a). *Genocide of Rwandan Tutsi, 1994.* Médecins Sans Frontières. (Médecins Sans Frontières Internal document). Geneva: The Médecins Sans Frontières International Movement.

MSF Speaking Out. (2014b). *Rwandan refugee camps in Zaire and Tanzania 1994-1995.* Médecins Sans Frontières. (Médecins Sans Frontières Internal document). Geneva: The Médecins Sans Frontières International Movement.

Narang, N. (2015). Assisting uncertainty: How Humanitarian Aid can inadvertently prolong Civil War. *International Studies Quarterly, 59*(1), 184–195.

Nnoli, O. (1978). *Self-reliance and foreign policy in Tanzania: The dynamics of the diplomacy of a new state, 1961-1971.* New York: NOK Publishers.

Nunn, N., & Qian, N. (2014). US food aid and civil conflict. *American Economic Review, 104*(6), 1630–1666.

Pogge, T. (2007a). Moral priorities for International Human Rights NGOs. In D. Bell & Jean Marc, C. (Eds.), *Ethics in action: The ethical challenges of international human rights nongovernmental organizations* (pp. 218–256). Cambridge: Cambridge University Press.

Pogge, T. (2007b). Assisting the global poor. In D. K. Chatterjee (Ed.), *The ethics of assistance: Morality and the distant needy* (pp. 260–289). Oxford: Cambridge University Press.

Prendergast, J., & Bennett, J. (1996). Frontline diplomacy. Humanitarian aid and conflict in Africa. *Disasters, 23*(1), 84–85.

Stockton, N. (2003). *Humanitarian values: Under siege from geopolitics.* Unpublished paper.

Terry, F. (1999). *Reconstituting whose social order? NGOs in disrupted states.* Paper presented at the conference entitled From Civil Strife to Civil Society: Civil-Military Cooperation in Disrupted States, Canberra, Australia.

Terry, F. (2002). *Condemned to repeat? The paradox of humanitarian action.* Ithaca, NY, London: Cornell University Press.

Terry, F., & Cordaro, B. (1994). *Message from MSF France coordinator in Ngara (Tanzania) to MSF France Programme manager.* (Médecins Sans Frontières Internal document). Genève: Médecins Sans Frontières International.

Vassall-Adams, G. (1994). *Rwanda: An agenda for international action.* Oxford: Oxfam Publications.

Von Pilar, U. (1999). *Humanitarian space under siege some remarks from an aid agency's perspective.* Background paper prepared for "the Symposium Europe and Humanitarian Aid – What Future? Learning from Crisis", Neuenahr, Germany.

Weiss, T. G. (1999). Principles, politics, and humanitarian action. *Ethics and International Affairs, 13*, 1–22.

Weiss, T.G., & Collins, C. (2000). *Humanitarian challenges and intervention.* 2nd ed. Routledge. https://doi.org/10.4324/9780429495182

Yéfime, Z. (1988). *A future preserved: International assistance to refugees.* Oxford: Pergamon Press.

3 Special relationships in conflict

Introduction

Despite humanitarian organisations' efforts to alleviate suffering and preserve human lives, the reality is that they sometimes increase the suffering of at least some affected populations. This is because their assistance can relieve belligerents' burden of sustaining conflicts and prolong the conflict. In this regard, humanitarian aid sometimes fails to serve its purpose of assisting the affected population and loses its innocent character. Furthermore, humanitarian organisations have been criticised for fuelling and prolonging conflicts by indirectly providing different forms of aid to belligerents, who are the main beneficiaries of relief aid. As a result, several practitioners, together with many scholars, have argued that aid should be withdrawn or reallocated, based on a consequentialist position, since the relief aid fails to maximise harm-reduction (Dallaire, 1998; Glennie, 2010; Lischer, 2005; Nunn & Qian, 2014; Polman & Waters, 2011; Terry, 2002; Väyrynen, 1999; Weiss, 1999).

It might seem that, intuitively, since humanitarian organisations are already there, they should stay and remain engaged with the affected population. The Humanitarian Exit Dilemma, therefore, can arise. Humanitarian organisations need to decide whether to withdraw and reallocate relief aid to maximise harm-reduction.[1] On the one hand, withdrawing aid will eliminate the possibility of assisting the needy affected population, but neither will aid exacerbate conflicts nor do more harm. On the other hand, staying will help the affected population but also perplex conflicts and lead to more harm than good overall. This chapter considers specifically one non-instrumental account to tackle the Humanitarian Exit Dilemma, which is humanitarian aid workers' special relationships with the affected population. It shows

DOI: 10.4324/9781003306696-3

how humanitarian aid workers' special relationships with the affected population may sometimes counteract humanitarian organisations' need to withdraw to reallocate assistance to maximise harm-reduction in conflicts. First, it demonstrates how aid workers in the field can, in effect, view the affected population as *having additional or special claims* on their assistance. Second, it shows that aid workers in the field can owe *associative duties* to the affected population to protect them from severe harm.

This view is referred to as the 'Associative Relationships Account' of what justifies the continued provision of assistance in the rest of this chapter. In line with this reasoning, this chapter concludes that humanitarian organisations should grant aid workers in the field the right to stay and remain engaged with the affected population. This is because of the moral significance of the affected population's special claims on the aid workers, and aid workers' associative duties to protect the affected population.

This chapter proceeds as follows. I begin by examining and analysing the formation of special relationships between humanitarian aid workers and those whom they assist in conflicts in the first section: I show that special relationships may or may not develop in the field, depending on the context. I then show in the following section that in situations where special relationships are not formed, humanitarian aid workers have *presumptively decisive reasons* to seek to form relationships when in the field.[2] Having shown that humanitarian aid workers do sometimes form personal relationships with the affected population, I demonstrate how these relationships can give rise to associative duties. Although I cannot offer a full theory of associative duties, I summarise the main schools of thought regarding how one's special relationship gives rise to one's associative duty, which is relevant to the justification of continued provision of assistance in conflicts. Particularly, the non-instrumentalist account in grounding special relationships' associative duties is considered.

I then elaborate on the Associative Relationships Account, which argues that our associative duties can sometimes justify our acting partially in protecting our friends or comrades against severe harm and hence sometimes outweigh our needs to maximise harm-reduction. Finally, I demonstrate how the Associative Relationships Account can be applied in practice, then consider and reject two potential objections to the Associative Relationships Account. A brief conclusion is given at the end of this chapter.

The formation of special relationships in conflicts

Evidence has shown that humanitarian aid workers sometimes form special relationships with the affected population (Agger et al., 1995; Beristain & Donà, 1998; Fuller, 2006; Heyse, 2006). For example, humanitarian aid workers often develop an intense closeness and a sense of shared experiences with the affected population due to the close, constant contact with them (Agger et al., 1995). Also, the process of assisting the affected population is considerably intense: the feeling of shared experiences with the affected population also creates a sense of closeness, which, as a result, creates a much closer relationship between the aid workers and the affected population than would be in normal working life (Eränen & Liebkind, 2003). Likewise, humanitarian aid workers in the field often consider the existing relationships between them and the affected population as "long-standing relationships" that are akin to friendships, which encourage humanitarian aid workers to work *with* the affected population rather than merely working *for* them (Stein, 2008, p.131).

The in-depth field report of Médecins Sans Frontières Holland (MSF Holland) also suggests that humanitarian organisations can develop close relationships with those they are assisting. It is found that a sense of solidarity is often developed within and during the development of personal relationships between aid workers of MSF Holland and the affected population (Fuller, 2006). For instance, many of MSF Holland's relief programmes converted into long-term assistance projects, which results in aid workers' high inclination to form close bonds with the affected population. It is also evident that aid workers of MSF Holland understand their relationships with the affected population as *committed relationships* akin to friendships rather than short-term or mere professional relationships (Fuller, 2006). For instance, some aid workers of MSF Holland stated that they committed to the specific affected population with whom they formed close bonds rather than aiding during a particular crisis. Others expressed their unwillingness to withdraw assistance from the affected population because of their close relationships with the affected population (Fuller, 2006).

Although MSF Holland's close relationships with those they are assisting cannot be taken as a universal case that can apply to every humanitarian organisation, it is nonetheless indicative. It shows that the kind of relationships the aid workers of MSF Holland have with the affected population is more than just professional. Other field research on MSF Holland also suggests that when aid workers of

MSF Holland have formed personal ties with the affected population, MSF Holland often bypasses the consequentialist consideration due to the personal ties (Heyse, 2006). In other words, aid workers of MSF Holland are inclined to disregard their need to maximise goal attainment against the lowest cost because they value and care about their ties with the affected population (Heyse, 2006).

Although different humanitarian organisations have different organisational structures and principles of humanitarian action, personal relationships with the affected population are often valued and considered essential for humanitarian aid workers (Carens, 2007). Even when aid workers of international non-governmental humanitarian organisations fail to form bonds with the affected population, aid workers of local non-governmental humanitarian organisations still often form close bonds with the affected population. For example, it is found that local humanitarian aid workers are more likely to relate to the traumatised population due to shared ethnic and cultural backgrounds (Musa & Hamid, 2008). Due to shared culture and experiences, local humanitarian aid workers identified with the affected population much more closely and more intensely than aid workers of INGOs (Cardozo et al., 2005). In short, although aid workers of international humanitarian organisations may fail to form bonds with the affected population, aid workers of local humanitarian organisations often form close bonds with the affected population.

Several reports also suggest that humanitarian aid workers often suffer from 'secondary traumatic stresses' due to their close relationships with the affected population (English, 1976; Figley, 1995; McFarlane, 2004; Musa & Hamid, 2008; Salama, 1997). The secondary traumatic stresses make humanitarian aid workers take in the affected population's misery and distress within themselves due to their close interaction with the affected population (English, 1976). Furthermore, evidence shows that at least 25% of humanitarian aid workers working for different humanitarian organisations severely suffer from secondary traumatic stress due to their close bonds with the affected population (Musa & Hamid, 2008).

Based on these findings, three points can be reasonably assumed. First, humanitarian aid workers of local or international humanitarian organisations can indeed form special relationships akin to friendships with those they are assisting, although this is not always the case. Second, humanitarian aid workers' psychological and emotional attachment often comes with close ties with the affected population. Third, failures to address the needs and interests of the subjects of these special relationships can profoundly affect humanitarian aid workers' well-being.

Now, at this point, one may still question the extent to which the relationships between humanitarian aid workers and the affected population can be viewed as friendships. My answer is this: although reports and field research do not directly show that humanitarian aid workers value their relationships with the affected population as friendships, research suggests that their relationships with the affected population are *like* friendships. For instance, it is evident that humanitarian aid workers in the field do not view their relationship with the affected population as a mere collegial relation, but, rather, more like friendships. This is because the interactions between humanitarian aid workers and the affected population constitute a particular interaction akin to friendships, which "involve expressed concern, self-revelation, and, more simply, shared activities" (Jeske, 1998, p.537).

In addition, unlike contracts or promises, the involved parties can identify and recognise friendships by observing their actions and attitudes towards each other. It follows that, even if the field reports do not explicitly show that the kind of relationships between the aid workers and the affected population are indeed friendships, it says little about the fundamental types of relationships between the aid workers and the affected population. After all, befriending someone does not always require one's explicit statement, such as I hereby befriend you.

To sum up, although the field reports discussed do not state that the kind of relationships between humanitarian aid workers in the field and the affected population are friendships, these relationships, nonetheless, share several fundamental elements of friendships, such as constant interactions, mutual understanding, and voluntary caring for each other. This is especially the case if we consider friendships encompassing trust, a sense of solidarity, shared interests, and engagement patterns. From this line of reasoning, we can logically reason that the relationships developed between humanitarian organisations and those they help are akin to friendships, if not friendships.

However, other field reports suggest that humanitarian aid workers may detach or are trained to detach from people they aim to assist despite the fact that several reports have shown that humanitarian aid workers do form special relationships with the affected population. Humanitarian aid workers may fail to form special relationships with the affected population in various situations (Autesserre, 2014; Harrell-Bond, 2002). For example, humanitarian aid workers may fail to form bonds with the affected population because they tend to live in their own personal and social circles, where they have little chance to interact with and integrate into the local population. Also, humanitarian aid workers are sometimes trained to detach from those they aim to assist because a distance to the affected population enables humanitarian aid workers to function in difficult conditions (Autesserre, 2014).

Although humanitarian aid workers may fail to form bonds with the affected population in some contexts, several studies have suggested that the *lack* of special relationships can, in effect, be extremely detrimental to aid effectiveness (Anderson et al., 2012; Autesserre, 2014; Coburn, 2011; Harrell-Bond, 2002; McWha, 2011). For example, it is found that the failure to form special relationships with the affected population can lead to a lack of understanding of local conditions, which can exacerbate the problems humanitarian aid workers aim to solve (Autesserre, 2014).

The failure to form special relationships with the affected population can also generate another detrimental consequence: it can lead to misconceptions and misunderstandings of those whom humanitarian aid workers aim to assist, which can undermine humanitarian aid workers' efforts (Autesserre, 2014). For instance, humanitarian aid workers could fail to influence local policy-making procedures because they do not have special relationships with the local population, which is deemed crucial to the local community (Coburn, 2011).

The failure to form special relationships with the affected population can also lead to other undesirable and contradictory results. It is found that humanitarian aid workers are more inclined to disrespect the affected population and treat the affected population as passive gift receivers when special relationships are lacking because aid workers can then perceive the affected population as nameless numbers rather than humans with faces, which dehumanises the affected population in an inhuman way (Harrell-Bond, 2002). This creates intensity and hostility in humanitarian aid workers' relationships with the affected population, which makes humanitarian aid workers more willing to act "crassly and sometimes cruelly" towards the affected population (Harrell-Bond, 2002, p.68).

In the long run, the failure to form meaningful personal relationships with the affected population makes humanitarian assistance to the affected population a mere act of "charity, rather than as a means of enabling refugees to enjoy their rights" (Harrell-Bond, 2002, pp.52–53). It further subordinates the affected population to mere aid receivers rather than human beings who also deserve dignity and rights. Eventually, humanitarian assistance fails to "uphold the dignity of the people they purport to serve, but positively violate their rights" (Harrell-Bond, 2002, pp.52–53).

By contrast, having special relationships with the affected population can sometimes provide humanitarian aid workers with a much more accurate perception of the challenges to the relief projects (Autesserre, 2014). For instance, it is found that good interaction between humanitarian aid workers and local populations can contribute to the relative success of ongoing humanitarian projects (McWha, 2011). However, humanitarian aid workers' working "in ways that develop respect and trust" with the affected population can help to create an efficient aid-distribution perception among the affected population (Anderson, Brown & Jean, 2012, p.144). This is because the affected population appreciates humanitarian aid workers' efforts to understand them and the contexts in which they live. Such appreciations help decrease the affected population's incentives to contest and resist humanitarian aid workers' efforts (Anderson, 2008).

Special relationships with the affected population are also crucial to promoting humanitarian aid workers' security, given that aid workers often work in conflicts (Autesserre, 2014). To sum up, in situations where special relationships are not formed, humanitarian aid workers should consider developing these relationships because it can help aid workers deliver aid more effectively and provide vital assistance.

This section has shown that humanitarian aid workers may or may not form personal relationships akin to friendships with the affected population. It also provides reasons why humanitarian aid workers may want to form relationships with the affected population. The next section discusses how special relationships, such as friendships or comradeships, can give rise to associative duties.

Grounding associative duties

Common-sense morality seems to understand our standing in special relationships with others as morally important in and of itself, be they comradeships, friendships, familial, compatriots, or professional relationships. It is widely held that several kinds of relationships can be the basis of special obligations that can induce our *associative duties* to those with whom we have such relationships. For those who see special relationships as intrinsically valuable, asking them to weigh their associative duties against their instrumental duties to promote the overall good outcome is counter-intuitive.

By contrast, consequentialists may view that one's reason to prioritise assisting those with whom one stands in special relationships provides no independent value to counteract one's duty to promote the overall good outcome. The consequentialist approach, however, fails to accommodate one's intuition that special bonds sometimes provide a *non-instrumental, independent* counterweight against our reasons to promote the overall good outcome. This is because common-sense morality seems to consider special relationships' moral significance for their own sake, not in virtue of other instrumentalist purposes that they can or may afford. The consequentialist approach also fails to recognise that special relationships are often valued and are deemed valuable because of *agent-centred* reasons, rather than agent-neutral reasons. For all these reasons discussed above, special relationships are often regarded as able to give rise to our associative duties.

This is not to argue that we always must act on our associative duties: to be clear, our associative duties, or special obligations, do not provide us all-things-considered reasons for action all the time. However, we have to recognise that our associative duties do provide us with presumptive decisive reasons for action, which is morally significant to us.

Attempts to ground special relationships' specific duties have appealed to two main opposing accounts: the instrumentalist account and the non-instrumentalist account of grounding associative duties (Lazar, 2013). The former justifies our associative duties by appealing to the kind of 'goods' special relationships are able to realise, while the latter justifies associative duties by appealing to special relationships' *independent moral import* and *non-instrumental values*.[3]

This chapter specifically considers the non-instrumentalist account of grounding associative duties because it provides persuasive reasons about why we should value special relationships and why we want to prioritise those with whom we have special relationships.

Special relationships are understood as being special or distinctive because they identify relations and associations between two particular groups that are not shared by all. Due to this particularity and exclusivity, special relationships are often valued for *agent-centred* reasons that are not shared by others and cannot be evaluated simply through agent-neutral reasons (Nagel, 1986; Parfit, 1984). To be more precise, agent-centred reasons to value our unique relationships are reasons that have an "essential reference" to us (Nagel, 1986, p.152). In contrast, agent-neutral reasons can only give us a general kind of motivation for actions.

Our agent-centred reasons to value our special relationships, to that extent, demand that we view those with whom we have special relationships as "capable of making additional claims" on us because our friends or comrades have provided us with *significant moral reasons* for action (Scheffler, 2002, p.101).

The claims our friends or associates can make on us, in this sense, are "beyond those that people in general can make", since our friends are themselves "a source of special claims" by virtue of these existing valuable relationships (Scheffler, 2002, p.101).[4]

People in general may make claims on us, and their needs and interests may also provide us with some reasons for action. Nevertheless, our friends or comrades can make *special* claims on us. This is because our friends or comrades provide us with "presumptively decisive" reasons for action. These reasons are *lacking* and would *not* have existed in the absence of these valuable relationships (Scheffler, 2002, p.100). This is similar to saying that our friends give us direct, weighty reasons for action, *independent* of their instrumental purposes. The claims our friends or comrades can make on us, therefore, can sometimes outweigh the claims people, in general, can make on us.

If this view is sound, we may be required to bear *special* duties to address the needs and interests of our friends or comrades to see them as having additional or special claims on us. Scheffler, for instance, proposes to see our friends as a source of our "special responsibilities" (2002, p.97). I share a similar view: our special relationships with our friends or associates can indeed ground our associative duties to protect them from severe harm.

Special relationships, be they colleagueship, friendships, or comradeships, all seem to be able to create *pro tanto duties* that demand we act in favour of our associates' and friends' needs and interests despite its arbitrary and contingent character; and this is because our participation in these special relationships is itself a sufficient source of specific rights and associative duties that are exclusive to the participants of that relationship. If we do not act partially towards the needs and interests of our friends or comrades, our participation in these special relationships will *not* be personal, *nor* will they be special (Cottingham, 1983; Kekes, 1981).

If we are not allowed to make room for reasonable partiality towards our comrades, friends, or compatriots, we fail to "take the complexity and richness of human relations and associations seriously" (Tan, 2005, p.167). Being our friends or comrades means that we have pro tanto duties to serve their interests and needs, which we would not have if there were no relationships. Based on our standing in such special relations to our associates and friends, "we are obligated to promote their interests in ways and degrees in which we are not obligated to promote the interests of persons who are not intimately related to us" (Jeske, 1998, p.530).

This is not to argue that we do not have duties to help people in general. Instead, I believe we owe general duties to all human beings by reason of our shared humanity (Murphy, 2011). General duties are duties that all moral beings "owe to other human beings simply qua status as human being" (Murphy, 2011, p.1028). These general duties hence are owed to all human beings. Although we may owe general duties to people in general, these duties are not always as stringent as the pro tanto duties we owe to our friends or comrades: our pro tanto duties to our associates (and thus acting partially to serve their interests and needs) is a *necessary condition* of being in any meaningful relationship. Our associative duties to assist our friends, in this sense, can thus take priority over our general duties to people in general sometimes.

However, depending on the context, I allow our associative duties to be overridden by other weightier moral reasons: although our friends or comrades provide us with morally compelling reasons to act, those reasons are "capable in principle of being outweighed or overridden" (Scheffler, 2002, p.100). Although our associative duties or special relationships arising from special relationships can at times provide sound justifications for our acting partially towards our associates and friends, these duties nevertheless need to be limited to certain general moral principles in order to avoid unjustified associate partiality (Tan, 2005).

Even if other weightier considerations may override our associative duties, they should *not* be dismissed easily. After all, if we accept that friendships, familial relationships, and other forms of special relationships have significant moral importance, we cannot reasonably reject that such significance can change the landscape of our moral reasoning and hence our decisions (Scheffler, 2002; Tan, 2005).

Having shown that our special relationships have non-instrumental values that can ground our associative duties to our friends and comrades, I now discuss the Associative Relationships Account: here I show how special relationships can justify our acting partially in protecting our friends against severe harm and sometimes outweigh our needs to maximise harm-reduction.

The 'Associative Relationships Account'

To motivate intuition, I present two case examples, the case of stranger X and the case of stranger group Z. Imagine that you come across the following situation. You are by three pools: Pool X, Pool Y, and Pool

Z. While Pool X and Pool Y contain the same number of drowning people (one person drowning in each pool) and the same number of capable swimmers available to save them (say three capable swimmers by each pool, on top of you), Pool Z has two drowning people. Let us now assume that stranger X, your friend Y, and strangers Z have the same chance of survival, given that they have the same chance of being saved. This is because there are equal numbers of capable swimmers by each pool. Also, let us assume that each capable swimmer has the same level of motivation to offer her help.

You are facing the following situation. There is a stranger, X, in Pool X who has a general claim on your positive duty of assistance. In Pool Y, there is your friend Yaris. You and Yaris both value your friendship, and both value it not merely for instrumental reasons but also its intrinsic importance. There are two people unknown to you in Pool Z; together, I call them 'strangers Z'. Strangers Z are unknown to you, but you and others can easily save them around the pool as a whole. In situations like this, who ought you to help? Stranger X, who is unknown to you; your friend Yaris, who has a special relationship with you; or strangers Z, with two lives at stake? My intuition suggests that we should help your friend Yaris, rather than stranger X or strangers Z.

The case of stranger X

Between helping your friend Yaris or stranger X, you may prioritise the needs and interests of Yaris over the needs and interests of X. In fact, I think you *ought to* prioritise the needs and interests of your friend Yaris. This is because the existing tie between you and Yaris rightly allows you to see Yaris as having an additional claim on your assistance in virtue of the relationship between you and Yaris. The fact that Yaris stands in a very special kind of relationship with you requires that you see Yaris as being able to make a special claim on you *beyond* those that people unknown to you can make in general, in the case X.

In particular, to say that Yaris has an additional claim or a special claim on your assistance is, in turn, to say that you have an associative duty—a pro tanto obligation—to protect Yaris from the severe harms with which the lack of assistance threatens Yaris. This makes your reasons to protect Yaris from severe harm *more pressing* than your reasons to help X. The existing valuable relationship between you and Yaris creates your pro tanto obligation to prioritise Yaris's needs and interests, which outweighs your positive duty to help X.

The case of strangers Z

In the case of strangers Z, your associative duties to Yaris may take precedence, although *not* always. To be more precise, your associative duty to protect Y from severe harm may sometimes outweigh your needs to maximise harm-reduction (in this case, helping strangers Z).

Unlike the case of stranger X, the case of strangers Z presents a more complex scenario. In the case of strangers Z, you may consider prioritising the needs and interests of strangers Z over Y, based on a consequentialist position to reduce as much harm as possible. This thought is appealing because you can save two people at once if you choose to help strangers Z; whereas you can only save one person if you choose to save Yaris. Although attractive, further reflections on the consequentialist approach led to doubts: your pro tanto obligations to protect your friends or comrades can sometimes outweigh your needs to maximise harm-reduction by raising two challenges to the consequentialist position.

The consequentialist approach demands that you maximise harm-reduction whenever possible, which leaves no room for your own personal commitments and agent-centred reasons. In the case of strangers Z, consequentialists will always demand that you prioritise strangers Z's needs and interests over Yaris's needs and interests. This can only be achieved by you ignoring the valuable relationship between you and Yaris. The consequentialist view, in this sense, is at odds with the interests of most moral agents, given that common-sense morality often allows or even demands that we bear greater costs to protect our friends against severe harm than we would if there were no relationships. In a sense, the fact that your agent-centred commitments are morally significant to you can provide a sound justification for you to act partially towards Yaris sometimes.

We also need to consider the normative weight of our associative duties, which are our pro tanto obligations. The consequentialist approach suggests that your needs to help strangers Z should always take precedence, which is way too demanding. Although saving strangers Z can maximise harm-reduction and produce the best outcome, it does not follow that the claims strangers Z can make on your assistance can always outweigh that of Yaris'. After all, the kind of claims strangers Z can make on you are *general* claims, which are not as weighty as the *special* claim of Yaris. Also, it is not clear that your general positive duties to strangers Z's should always override your pro tanto obligations to Yaris just because strangers Z are greater in number. Hence, it is not obvious that our need to maximise harm-reduction should always precede our associative duties to protect our friends or comrades from severe harm. It may even be the case that the associative duties you owe to limited numbers of specific persons are weightier than the general positive duties you have to a larger number of people.

If we adopt the consequentialist approach, a worrying situation may occur: the moral significance of special relationships can be dismissed insofar as we multiply the number of people we could have helped or aggregate the amounts of harm we could have mitigated. The consequentialist approach risks ignoring that our standing in particular relation to others, our personal commitments, and our agent-centred reasons do matter to us and should matter to us. The moral significance of our special relationships, to that extent, provides us with compelling moral reasons to counteract other duties, such as our pro tanto duties to maximise harm-reduction.

The next step is to show that the threat of conflicts can engage humanitarian aid workers' associative duties with which the lack of assistance threatens the affected populations. In what follows, I consider specifically how our associative duties are transferred to humanitarian aid workers assisting those with whom they have special relationships. I show how humanitarian aid workers' associative duties to the affected populations justify their continued engagement.

Associative Relationships Account applied in humanitarian action

Relationships between humanitarian aid workers and those they assist often make humanitarian aid workers see themselves as owing the affected population *additional* duties. In particular, the findings suggest that humanitarian aid workers often value their relationships with the affected population for intrinsic rather than instrumental reasons.

When facing the Humanitarian Exit Dilemma, humanitarian organisations may consider withdrawing assistance from the affected population to use scarce aid more conducive to maximising harm-reduction. However, the value of this line of action can be outweighed by other reasoning, which includes the concern for the affected population's *special claims on assistance*, and *the associative duties* humanitarian aid workers owe to the affected population.

The affected population can make special claims on humanitarian aid workers because the existing relationships between the two parties have a non-instrumental moral significance both aid workers and the affected population have reasons to value and the actual value. Correspondingly, humanitarian aid workers have associative duties to prioritise the needs of those with special relationships because such relationships create humanitarian aid workers' pro tanto obligations, which demand that they place additional attention on their needs compared to people in general. The Associative Relationships Account, to that extent, provides morally weighty reasons for humanitarian organisations to stay and remain engaged with the affected population rather than withdrawing assistance to maximise harm-reduction.

To demand that humanitarian aid workers disregard the needs and interests of those with whom they have special relationships for the reasons of consequential rationale will otherwise overlook the *presumptive moral force* of the existing valuable relationships. When special relationships are formed in the field, humanitarian organisations have morally significant reasons not to withdraw their assistance in fields. The special claims the affected population have on the aid workers and the created pro tanto obligations they owe to the affected population provide humanitarian organisations with morally weighty reasons to stay and remain engaged with the affected population.

One may simply question why the relationships between humanitarian aid workers and those they are assisting fall into the category of special when such relationships appear to fall into professional relationships.

My answer to this doubt draws on empirical findings. Several reports and investigations have suggested that humanitarian aid workers' relationships with the affected population entail more friendship-like elements than professional relationships. For instance, it is shown that the kind of relationship between the aid workers of MSF Holland and the affected population is a distinctive kind of relationship grounded in a concern for personal commitment, trust, mutual caring, and respect.

Professional relationships, however, often exclude, or even forbid, the core elements friendships possess. For example, if we consider professional relationships, such as relationships between doctors and patients, we may find that some core elements of friendships are not encouraged to be formed or are forbidden to be formed. A professional relationship can be defined as an association between the involved parties based on providing service to people in an appropriate manner by the professionals, which entails setting borders or limits between the professionals and the patients. In professional relationships, the involved parties do not develop or are forbidden to develop a concern of mutual caring and personal commitments as in the way special relationships require. Professional relationships, rather, possess a "technician" like quality, which is about "consistent application of rules and procedures" and professional skills "not to be deterred by tough choices or emotional engagement" (Hopgood, 2008, p.114). Professional relationships, to that extent, have at their core concerns about performance, as well as concerns about service delivery.

By contrast, humanitarian assistance has concerns about humanitarian imperative and human dignity at its core. This means that humanitarian organisations do *not* see their humanitarian efforts as merely service delivery but as a genuine and intimate concern for the dignity and well-being of the affected population, which is rooted in humanitarian engagement (Hopgood, 2008). In the long run, if humanitarian work is to be humane or humanitarian, it should be of humanity, not just efficiency, effectiveness, or professionalism (Harrell-Bond, 2002; Hopgood, 2008). The nature of humanitarian work differs fundamentally from other professional occupations precisely because it requires so much more than a simple meeting of needs. It requires significant humanitarian concern that consists of a caring relationship with the affected population, aid workers standing in solidarity with the affected population, and mutual dependence of the subjects of the relationship (Hopgood, 2008). This is as long as humanitarian aid workers can maintain such humanitarian concerns consistent with adequate care for themselves.

Although some particular professional relationships, such as doctors-patients, seem to entail mutual caring and specific commitment, such commitment and mutual caring are impersonal and cease to exist when the duties of care attached to their roles are fulfilled. On the contrary, the kind of mutual caring and personal commitment in friendships persist insofar as the friendships exist. There is a significant difference between caring and commitment in professional and committed personal relationships.

One may also argue that humanitarian aid workers are working in a public realm, and because of this, they are required to be impartial when delivering aid. Otherwise, they risk undermining their own principles of neutrality and impartiality.

My response is this: although humanitarian aid workers do occupy roles in which a certain kind of impartiality is demanded of them (regarding the interests of affected populations for whom they have responsibility), they are not like a judge, teacher, or tax officer working in the public institution. In addition, humanitarian organisations are non-governmental organisations with distinct organisational principles that endorse different virtues, rules, guidelines, mandates, and codes of conduct. To that extent, humanitarian organisations occupy positions in which *different kinds of virtues* are demanded of them with regards to the interests of affected populations to whom they have responsibility. Impartiality is just one of the many. This unique feature of humanitarian organisations (non-governmental, non-profitable, and voluntary) hence places humanitarian aid workers in a position between individuals and public officers. For example, humanitarian aid workers are *not* required to be impartial in the same sense as a judge or a tax officer working in a public institution.

This can be explained by first considering the following question: are there any specific impersonal criteria that demand humanitarian aid workers not to show personal commitments by virtue of their job? The answer, as I understand it, is no. Although humanitarian aid workers may be required to be impartial, they are required to follow this impersonal criterion only to the extent that they distribute aid regardless of aid recipients' race, gender, religion, nationality, and social background. However, being impartial does not require that humanitarian aid workers treat those with special relationships with them as having *no* moral significance. The demand for the impartiality of humanitarian aid workers is fulfilled as long as they make no discrimination based on nationality, race, religious beliefs, class, or political opinions when delivering their assistance.

If the reasoning is sound, the kind of impartiality required in humanitarian assistance actually "permits the impartial person to be judgemental—albeit not gratuitously so, but in line with agreed values" (Slim, 1997, p.349). The kind of impartiality demanded in the humanitarian sphere should leave sufficient room and adequate space for humanitarian aid workers to weigh their agent-relative values against other values when distributing aid. In fact, it is found that some humanitarian agencies encourage their aid workers to form special relationships with those they help (such as MSF Holland), while others choose to stand in solidarity and act partially towards those they help (such as Norwegian People's Aid), to reflect their core belief in solidarity and appropriateness.

When considering what is required when delivering aid, one must ask, are there rules determining how much help per conflict victim should be received? Also, are humanitarian organisations under a specific duty to apply these rules *equally to all*? If the answer is not absolute, one may agree that humanitarian aid workers are similar to individuals and should be given room to fulfil their own commitments that they deem worthy of pursuit. After all, it is important to bear in mind that different humanitarian organisations have *different priorities* at their core.

Conclusion

Distributing humanitarian assistance in extreme emergencies is often discussed in the language of effectiveness and efficiency. However, it is seldom discussed in a way that seriously takes the perspective of humanitarian aid workers, the affected population, and their special relationships. This chapter considers humanitarian aid workers' close ties with the affected population to address this gap.

Although it is important to consider consequences and their value in the humanitarian sphere, consequences are only one value amongst all other values. Humanitarian organisations should consider consequences as an important value but no more than an important value amongst all other values. Other non-consequentialist values also demand humanitarian organisations' particular attention. Humanitarian agencies have to see the consequence as a value that can be traded off or outweighed by other values. Only in so doing can one recognise and acknowledge other morally significant values and consider the moral importance of consequences.

The consequentialist approach can be problematic in a humanitarian context because it risks reducing all values (affection, commitment, feeling, and desire) to utilitarian considerations. This leaves no room for non-consequential interests that humanitarian aid workers genuinely care about and further disassociates one from his/her moral feeling.

Although humanitarian organisations may weigh the consequentialist account as a good enough reason to withdraw their current projects, it is sometimes justifiable and permissible to remain engaged with those they know and care about in the face of the Humanitarian Exit Dilemma. Humanitarian organisations should not simply suppose that the concern for consequences is all that should matter to them. Even if humanitarian organisations have duties of utility to promote as much net good as they can, these duties should "occupy only a portion" of their moral reasoning (Norman, 1995, p.106). After all, humanitarian age organisations also have to consider other more specific responsibilities that arise from their special standing with those they know and care about, which also "compete for space" in their humanitarian practice (Norman, 1995, p.106). In such situations, one may as well reason that it is morally preferable for humanitarian organisations to save those who are small in number but have significant ties to them rather than a larger population.

This chapter suggested a Non-Consequentialist Approach for humanitarian organisations. It proposed the Associative Relationships Account to tackle the Humanitarian Exit Dilemma. It examined and discussed the significant moral importance and the positive perspectives of special relationships in conflicts. It first showed that special relationships have independent values, stemming from the importance of special relationships with humanitarian aid workers and personal commitments to the affected population. It then established that these special relationships had provided humanitarian aid workers with weighty agent-centred reasons to stay and remain engaged with the affected population, which grounded humanitarian aid workers' associative duties to act partially to serve the needs of the affected population. Finally, it justified humanitarian organisations' continued provision of assistance. Overall, the Associative Relationships Account argued that humanitarian aid workers' special relationships with the affected population could *sometimes* override humanitarian organisations' needs to maximise harm-reduction while acknowledging that humanitarian aid workers' associative duties to the affected population are *not* absolute.

Notes

1 The maximisation of harm-reduction is the ability to reallocate aid to other places where more harm can be mitigated, and more people can be helped.
2 The associations between humanitarian aid workers and the affected population might vary. I do not wish to say that humanitarian aid workers always have relationships akin to friendship with the affected population. Rather, in situations where humanitarian aid workers form relationships akin to friendships with those they are assisting, aid workers have associative duties towards those with whom they are thus associated.
3 Seth Lazar uses the term 'teleological' to refer to the instrumentalist justification of associative duties and 'nonteleological' to refer to the noninstrumentalist justification of associative duties (2013).
4 The fit to Scheffler's account is not perfect: I only claim that the relationship between aid workers and those they assist might not be quite a friendship but something akin to it.

References

Agger, I., Vuk, S., & Mimica, J. (1995). *Theory and practice of psycho-social projects under war conditions in Bosnia-Herzegovina and Croatia.* European Community Humanitarian Office (ECHO).
Anderson, M. (2008). The giving receiving relationship: Inherently unequal? In S. Hidalgo, López-Claros, L. Altinger (Eds.), *The Humanitarian Response Index 2008: Donor accountability in humanitarian action* (pp. 97–105). London; Madrid: DARA; Palgrave Macmillan.

Anderson, M., Brown, D., & Jean, I. (2012). *Time to listen: Hearing people on the receiving end of international aid.* Cambridge: CDA Collaborative Learning Projects.

Autesserre, S. (2014). *Peaceland conflict: Resolution and the everyday politics of international intervention.* Cambridge: Cambridge University Press.

Beristain, C. M., & Donà, G. (1998). *Psychology in humanitarian assistance.* Luxembourg: Official Publications of the European Communities.

Cardozo, B., Holtz, T., Kaiser, R., Gotway, A., Ghitis, F., Toomey, E., & Salama, P. (2005). The mental health of expatriate and Kosovar Albanian humanitarian aid workers. *Disasters, 29*(2), 152–170.

Carens, J. (2007). The problem of doing good in a world that isn't: Reflections on the ethical challenges facing INGOs. In D. Bell & J. Coicaud (Eds.), *Ethics in action* (pp. 257–272). Cambridge: Cambridge University Press.

Coburn, N. (2011). *Bazaar politics power and pottery in an Afghan Market Town.* Stanford, CA: Stanford University Press.

Cottingham, J. (1983). Ethics and impartiality. *Philosophical Studies: An International Journal for Philosophy in the Analytic Tradition, 43*(1), 83–99.

Dallaire, R. (1998). The end of innocence: Rwanda 1994. In J. Moore (Ed.), *Hard choice: Moral dilemmas in humanitarian intervention* (pp. 71–97). Lanjam, MD: Rowman & Littlefield.

English, O. S. (1976). The emotional stress of psychotherapeutic practice. *Journal of the American Academy of Psychoanalysis, 4*(2), 191–201.

Eränen, L., & Liebkind, K. (1993). Coping with disaster: The helping behaviour of communities and individuals. In J. P. Wilson & B. Raphael (Eds.), *International handbook of traumatic stress syndromes* (pp. 957–964). New York: Plenum Press.

Figley, C. F. (1995). Compassion fatigue as secondary traumatic stress disorder: An overview. In C. F. Figley (Ed.), *Compassion Fatigue: Coping with Secondary Traumatic Stress Disorder in Those Who Treat the Traumatized* (pp. 1–20). Medina, NY: Brunner.

Fuller, L. (2006). Justified commitments? Considering resource allocation and fairness in Médecins Sans Frontières-Holland. *Developing World Bioethics, 6*(2), 59–70.

Glennie, J. (2010). More aid is not the answer. *The Journal of Contemporary World Affairs, 109*(727), 205.

Harrell-Bond, B. (2002). Can humanitarian work with refugees be humane?. *Human Rights Quarterly, 24*(1), 51–85.

Heyse, L. (2006). *Choosing the lesser evil: Understanding decision making in humanitarian aid NGOs.* Aldershot: Ashgate Publishing Limited.

Hopgood, S. (2008). Saying no to Wal-Mart? Money and morality in professional humanitarianism. In M. Barnett & T. Weiss (Eds.), *Humanitarian in question: Politics, power, ethics* (pp. 73–97). London: Cornell University Press.

Jeske, D. (1998). Families, friends, and special obligations. *Canadian Journal of Philosophy, 28*(4), 527–555.

Kekes, J. (1981). Morality and impartiality. *American Philosophical Quarterly, 18*(4), 295–303.

Lazar, S. (2013). Associative duties and the ethics of killing in war. *Journal of Practical Ethics, 1*(1), 1–31.

Lischer, S. K. (2005). *Dangerous sanctuaries: Refugee camps, civil war, and the dilemmas of humanitarian aid.* Cornell University Press. https://www.jstor.org/stable/10.7591/j.cttltm7g8v

McFarlane, C. A. (2004). Risks Associated with the Psychological Adjustment of Humanitarian Aid Workers. *Australasian Journal of Disaster and Trauma Studies,* 1.

McWha, I. (2011). The roles of, and relationships between, expatriates, volunteers, and local development workers. *Development in Practice, 21*(1), 29–40.

Murphy, S.P. (2011). Special obligations. In: D.K. Chatterjee, (Eds.), *Encyclopedia of Global Justice.* Dordrecht: Springer. https://doi.org/10.1007/978-1-4020-9160-5_390

Musa, S. A., & Hamid, A. (2008). Psychological problems among aid workers operating in Darfur. *Social Behaviour and Personality, 36*(3), 407–416.

Nagel, T. (1986). *The view from nowhere.* Oxford: Oxford University Press.

Norman, R. (1995). *Ethics, killing & war.* Cambridge: Cambridge University Press.

Nunn, N., & Qian, N. (2014). US food aid and civil conflict. *American Economic Review, 104*(6), 1630–1666.

Parfit, D. (1984). *Reasons and persons.* Oxford: Oxford University Press.

Polman, L., & Waters, L. (2011). *The crisis caravan: What's wrong with humanitarian aid?* New York: Picador.

Salama, P. (1999). The psychological health of relief workers: Some practical suggestions. *Humanitarian Exchange Magazine, 15*(10).

Scheffler, S. (2002). *Boundaries and allegiances: Problems of justice and responsibility in liberal thought.* Oxford: Oxford University Press.

Slim, H. (1997). Doing the right thing: Relief agencies, moral dilemmas and moral responsibility in political emergencies and war. *Disasters, 21*(3), 244–257.

Stein, J. (2008). Humanitarian organizations: Accountable—Why, to whom, for what, and how? In M. Barnett & T. Weiss (Eds.), *Humanitarian in question: Politics, power, ethics* (pp. 124–142). Ithaca, NY, London: Cornell University Press.

Tan, K. C. (2005). Cosmopolitan impartiality and patriotic partiality. *Canadian Journal of Philosophy Supplementary Volume, 31,* 165–192.

Terry, F. (2002). *Condemned to repeat? The paradox of humanitarian action.* Ithaca, NY, London: Cornell University Press.

Väyrynen, R. (1999). More questions than answers: Dilemmas of humanitarian action. *Peace and Change, 24*(2), 172–196.

Weiss, T. G. (1999). Principles, politics, and humanitarian action. *Ethics & International Affairs, 13,* 1–22.

4   Vulnerability and distinct obligation

Introduction

The Humanitarian Exit Dilemma often arises when humanitarian assistance generates an overall negative, rather than positive, impact on affected populations all things considered. As established in Chapter 2, there are five crucial ways that the Humanitarian Exit Dilemma can manifest in conflicts, one of which is undermining local coping strategies and reinforcing wartime economies. Under these conditions, affected populations are often made more vulnerable and more inclined to depend on external aid and assistance. Several aid practitioners, together with many theorists, hence have this fear that a vicious circle of aid dependency is created and that affected populations' aid-dependency syndrome and dependency mentality are further developed (Assal, 2008; Bartle, 2012; Christoplos, 2004; De Waal, 1997; Fineman, 2001; Hassan, 1996; Knack, 2000; Swift et al., 2002). The Humanitarian Exit Dilemma manifested in this way can create the ethical predicament of creating affected populations' dependence on aid.

Although affected populations' capacities to meet needs are undermined, aid also enables them to meet basic needs that they will otherwise fail to meet without external assistance. Therefore, while humanitarian organisations have good reasons to withdraw their assistance, they might want to stay and remain engaged with those relying on aid for other morally weighty reasons.

To that extent, this chapter addresses the following ethical predicament in deciding whether continuing aid is appropriate: should humanitarian organisations stay and remain engaged with current affected populations, or should they leave and reallocate the aid to other places where more people can be helped and where aid does not undermine local economies? In answering this question, this chapter

DOI: 10.4324/9781003306696-4

focuses specifically on one of the reasons to stay and remain engaged with current affected populations. This is humanitarian organisations' *distinct obligation* to those urgently depending on aid.

This chapter argues that humanitarian organisations should stay and remain engaged in the face of the Humanitarian Exit Dilemma because of (i) current affected populations' (current aid recipients) *additional vulnerability* and (ii) humanitarian organisations' causal responsibility in contributing to *the harm of unique dependence* to current aid recipients.

To begin, I elaborate on how victims (in this context, aid dependents) come to depend on aid in times of conflict. I introduce the dependence theory by Scott M. James, which entails a specific view of the dependence situation, namely the 'Unique Dependence Argument'. The view is relevant to individuals' dependence on aid (2007). I then develop and elaborate on my own 'Distinct Dependence Account' to address the ethical predicament noted above.

Two clarifications should be made before beginning. First, this chapter is not concerned with the impact of aid dependence or the possible means of eradicating aid dependence. This is because considering all the possible impacts of aid dependence would obscure this book's focus. This chapter focuses on the fact that relief aid is often *necessary* and *inevitable* in conflicts, despite its possible negative impacts.[1]

Second, this chapter abstracts and generalises features of aid dependence; hence it must be remembered that the impact of aid dependence (and the degree of dependence on aid) varies from one case to another (Hammock & Lautze, 1996). For example, in parts of Ethiopia where relief aid has become a regular event, the impact of relief aid is likely to be more visible compared to places where relief aid is a rarer event (Harvey & Lind, 2005). Contrarily, in areas where relief aid is viewed as something unexpected that cannot be counted on, such as Northern Kenya, aid dependence is less likely to occur.

On affected populations' dependence on aid

Several findings indicate that relief aid delivered in the context of extreme emergencies and fragile livelihoods can create dependence amongst those who receive aid (Assal, 2008; Bartle, 2012; Christoplos, 2004; De Waal, 1997; Fineman, 2001; Hassan, 1996; Knack, 2000; Swift et al., 2002). Humanitarian assistance can create victims' dependence on aid in several ways. For instance, humanitarian assistance can create victims' dependence on aid when it undermines local economies: according to the report of Grassroots International, several United States Agency for International Development (USAID) funded aid programmes were found to undermine local initiatives and create aid dependency in Haiti, due to its focus on short-term offers of food and employment (Richardson, 1997). Humanitarian assistance can also create victims' dependence on aid when it is provided for a period of time on a regular basis: in Northern Kenya, the provision of relief aid was found to encourage some Northern Kenyan communities to sedentarise during periods of adequate rainfall while anticipating assistance during drought due to the presence of aid (Swift et al., 2002). Finally, humanitarian assistance can create victims' dependence on aid when it becomes the only means for victims of conflicts to sustain themselves: Jean-Nicolas Marti (2012), the head of the ICRC regional delegation for Mali and Niger, states that people in the Northern part of Mali continue to suffer from the consequence of armed conflicts. Consequently, many have no choice but to depend solely on relief aid for survival.

Crises entail extreme levels of vulnerability and risk. In a sense, dependence on aid is a defining feature of the urgent need for humanitarian assistance. When crises undermine the ability of victims to meet their essential subsistence needs, they have to depend on external assistance. In addition, humanitarian organisations are often the only agencies capable of assisting needy victims. This is largely due to political reasons: third parties such as state actors and governmental organisations are often denied access to the affected populations because belligerents often consider their humanitarian efforts a tool to undermine their own power (Abiew, 2012; Jessen-Petersen, 2011). This often makes victims depend solely on humanitarian organisations' assistance. From the humanitarian organisations' perspective, they are often the only actors in a position to help needy victims.

A 'unique dependent' relationship between humanitarian organisations and current aid recipients can arise. The core characteristic of this relationship lies in that humanitarian organisations are the only ones who can assist the current aid recipients. This kind of dependent relationship is unique, given that it is formed in the way that an agent is uniquely dependent on you while you have complete control over her fate. Due to the uniqueness of this relationship, you are required to bear what is called a 'unique obligation' to assist her (James, 2007).

Grounding affected populations' unique status of dependence

James defines unique dependence as a specific kind of dependence that generates your unique obligation to a determinate individual who relies on you and only you for help. James develops the Unique Dependence Argument with the following thought experiment: if a child drowning in a pond you happen upon is uniquely dependent on you, your refusal to help her guarantees her imminent death. Unlike the child in the pond, distant people who need humanitarian relief assistance are not uniquely dependent on you. Your refusal to help them does not necessarily guarantee their imminent deaths; instead, you simply fail to be as good as you could be. Therefore, you do those distant needy people no wrong if you do not contribute to humanitarian relief efforts. After all, you are not morally required to provide aid: you may do it as a supererogatory action. However, if you fail to respond to the need of the drowning child who is uniquely dependent on you, you fail your unique obligation to her, thus acting wrongly towards her (James, 2007).

In the hypothetical example, the drowning child is distinctly dependent on you. In contrast, distant needy people are not: you have complete control over the child's survival because your refusal to help her will assure her imminent death. The child is, in this sense, uniquely dependent on you. In contrast, you have no control over the situation of distant needy people because your refusal to help them does not assure their imminent deaths. Their imminent deaths will occur if and only if all actors, including other third parties, fail to act. In this sense, distant needy people are not uniquely dependent.

Also, you and distant needy people are far from each other, making it difficult for you to have complete control over their situation, and the outcome hence has a fundamental indeterminacy. The proximity between the givers and receivers of aid plays a role in determining the unique relations. For an agent to be uniquely dependent on you, she has to be determinable (James, 2007). The drowning child, for instance, is a determinate individual because you can clearly identify whom you might or might not have saved had you taken a (further) action. However, distant needy people often consist of indeterminable individuals because you cannot identify whom you might or might not have saved had you taken further action.

While James's Unique Dependence Argument considers the unique dependence relationship in a one-off situation only, this chapter is concerned with the unique dependence relationship resulting from other agents' causal contributions in a situation of continuous conflict. This difference necessitates the development of my account, the Distinct Dependence Account, which modifies James' dependence theory to answer the Humanitarian Exit Dilemma properly.

The 'Distinct Dependence Account'

As noted earlier, third parties such as state actors and international organisations are often denied access to victims by belligerents because of their political nature. In contrast, humanitarian organisations are often granted access to the affected population because belligerents regard them as beneficial to their political ends and therefore welcome humanitarian organisations' presence (Abiew, 2012; Jessen-Petersen, 2011). For instance, warring parties often consider humanitarian organisations 'useful' because they can play refugee cards to obtain aid resources and protection while planning further violence (Väyrynen, 1999).

In this situation, the affected population is often dependent on humanitarian organisations and can *only* depend on humanitarian organisations for help. Hence, there is a unique dependence relationship between humanitarian organisations and the affected population in question. The affected population are often made even more dependent because humanitarian assistance has undermined local coping strategies and helped maintain wartime economies. This indicates that the affected population is uniquely dependent on aid due largely to humanitarian organisations' operations.

Although humanitarian organisations may be tempted to withdraw their assistance from current aid recipients to use scarce aid in a way more conducive to the overall consequences, the value of this line of action can be overridden by other considerations, which include (1) the concern for current aid recipients' additional vulnerability, and (2) humanitarian organisations' significant causal contribution to current aid recipients' unique dependence on aid. I call this the 'Distinct Dependence Account'.

These two crucial claims of the Distinct Dependence Account can provide humanitarian organisations with sufficient reasons to stay and remain engaged with current aid recipients. I discuss the two crucial claims of the Distinct Dependence Account in turn. I first discuss current aid recipients' additional vulnerability. I then discuss humanitarian organisations' causal responsibility in causing the harm of unique dependence to current aid recipients.

Current aid recipients' vulnerability and need

Current aid recipients who are uniquely dependent on humanitarian organisations are often more vulnerable and are thus more in need of humanitarian organisations' assistance than other needy people, provided that they are not uniquely dependent on humanitarian organisations.

Vulnerability entails a severe degree of neediness. It also implies that specific actors are "capable of exercising some effective choice over whether to cause or to avert the threatened harm" (Goodin, 1985, p.112). Vulnerability is to be understood as 'vulnerability to' some specific person. This view reflects the core characteristic of a unique dependence relationship. Once a unique dependence relationship is identified between you and another person, the dependent party will become extremely vulnerable to harm. This is because the non-dependent party alone can determine whether to prevent imminent harm. It is a concern for another moral being's vulnerability that demands you act with due regard for the consequences of your actions and decisions.

Although other needy people (considered here as not uniquely dependent on humanitarian organisations) can also be vulnerable and need help, their vulnerability is not as pressing as current aid recipients. This is because other needy people are not dependent on humanitarian organisations like current aid recipients. While there might be other capable agencies that are able to come to other needy people's aid, current aid recipients can depend only on humanitarian organisations' help. In other words, other needy people are more likely to survive without humanitarian organisations' help. By contrast, current aid recipients can only rely on you: if humanitarian organisations fail to act, there is no other possible way for current aid recipients to survive.

Like the case of Northern Mali, those currently relying on aid are often uniquely dependent on humanitarian organisations. If humanitarian organisations withdraw, refugees in Northern Mali will be more vulnerable than refugees in, for example, Bhutan, who do *not* rely on humanitarian organisations as the only means of survival and are, therefore, not uniquely dependent on humanitarian organisations' help.[2] Hence, compared to other needy populations who are less likely to be as vulnerable as current aid dependents, current aid dependents have weightier claims for humanitarian organisations' help.

It is important to note that other (distant) victims can be as uniquely dependent as current aid recipients. This is a crucial point to consider, given that other distant victims who are not adjacent to humanitarian organisations may, in some rare cases, be uniquely dependent on humanitarian organisations. Accordingly, in situations where both current aid recipients and other distinct victims are uniquely dependent, humanitarian organisations' obligations to help both groups are equally weighty and equally demanding. There is, therefore, a need to take other factors into account, such as humanitarian organisations' *causal role* in contributing to current aid recipients' unique dependence on aid to justify their decision to stay when confronted with a Humanitarian Exit Dilemma.

So far, I have shown that humanitarian organisations can be held responsible for distant victims' well-being for the same reason they have for current aid recipients. What remains unclear is whether humanitarian organisations should prioritise helping distant victims or current aid recipients. It does not help humanitarian organisations answer the difficult question of whom to assist in these situations. Therefore, it is necessary to consider other morally important factors other than one's unique dependence to determine whom to assist. To address this quandary properly, the Distinct Dependence Account considers humanitarian organisations' *causal contribution* to current aid recipients' unique dependence.

Causation and harm

Humanitarian organisations may have a unique obligation to both distant victims and current aid recipients. However, humanitarian organisations often *contribute* to current aid recipients' unique dependence on aid. It seems much harder for humanitarian organisations to contribute to distant needy victims' unique dependence on aid (given that humanitarian organisations' actual presence in the affected areas is required to undermine local economies and create dependence). In this sense, humanitarian organisations' obligations to assist current aid recipients are increased and magnified because of their causal role in causing the harm of unique dependence to current aid recipients.

I argue that humanitarian organisations have a 'distinct obligation' to current aid recipients. This distinct obligation is more demanding than humanitarian organisations' unique obligation or humanitarian organisations' general duty of assistance. To illustrate this and to motivate one's intuition, consider first the *Wrong Swimming Strokes* case.

Wrong Swimming Strokes: Imagine that you pass a pond on your route to the campus. One morning, you notice that a child has fallen in and appears to be drowning. You walk towards the child and recognise her: you had seen the child in the swimming pool once before and taught her how to swim. You knew that once you had taught her how to swim, she would rely on those swimming strokes. She would not seek out other teachers once you had taught her. Though no fault of your own, you voluntarily demonstrated the swimming strokes incorrectly. You were taught these swimming strokes once. Unbeknownst to you, although they enable you to swim through floating because you are extremely fat, they would not work for a much smaller and thinner person. As a result of you teaching the girl, she cannot be self-reliant in the pond and is now in need of your assistance to keep her from drowning.

Now consider the *Drowning Child* case: Imagine that your route to campus takes you past a shallow pond. One morning, you notice that a child has fallen in and appears to be drowning. It would be easy to pull the child out, but it would also mean that you get your clothes wet and muddy, meaning you will miss your class (Singer, 1972, 1997).

Wrong Swimming Strokes presents a case where the child is uniquely dependent on you because you have caused her unique dependence on you. In contrast, *Drowning Child*[3] presents a case where the child is uniquely dependent on you only because of a coincidence (you were in the right place at the right time), regardless of your voluntary choice, knowledge, and causal relationship. Intuitively, you should be required to bear a very special kind of obligation to help the child in *Wrong Swimming Strokes*. This is because you committed yourself to teaching her how to swim and significantly contributed to her unique dependence. You have prevented her from learning the correct swimming strokes by teaching her the wrong ones. In the *Drowning Child* case, we are inclined to think that, although you also have a duty to help the child, this duty is not as demanding as the duty incurred in the case of *Wrong Swimming Strokes*.

The fundamental difference between *Drowning Child* and *Wrong Swimming Strokes* is that, in the former case, the child is solely dependent on you by chance. In contrast, the child is uniquely dependent on you largely because of your actions in the latter case. Surely your obligation to help the child to whom you have caused the harm of unique dependence is increased and exacerbated (because of your causal role in causing that particular harm) compared to the obligation you have to the child who is suffering the harm of unique dependence only because of his bad luck.

Consider another analogous case to draw further on our common-sense intuitions:

Two Dependent Children: There are two close-by shallow ponds on your route to the campus. Though shallow, a child may fall into either pond and drown. One morning, you see two children falling into each pond. Both children appear to be drowning. You walk towards the child drowning in one of the ponds, recognising him as Fred. You saw Fred in the swimming pool once, and you happened to teach Fred the wrong swimming strokes, which has now made him unable to save himself. While you can recognise Fred, the other child who fell into the pond is a stranger to you. It would be equally easy to pull Fred or another child out. However, you only have time to save one of them from drowning.

In the *Two Dependent Children* case, it seems intuitive that you have a weightier reason to save Fred over another child, leading you to prioritise saving Fred, to whom you have taught the wrong swimming stroke. This is not to say that you do not have a duty to help another child. It is merely that the reason to save Fred is more compelling and weightier. In other words, causal relations play a significant role in your duty to other individuals, especially under conditions where you have significantly contributed to the harm of unique dependence. Although both Fred and another child are uniquely dependent on you in the *Two Dependent Children* case, Fred has a weightier claim for your help. We think your duties are increased, magnified, or exacerbated if you have caused harm to the person in question. Consequently, it captures the intuition that your obligation to the person you cause harm is more demanding than your obligation to another person merely through luck. When you have contributed significantly to causing the harm of unique dependence, you have a 'distinct obligation' to prioritise taking care of those to whom you cause harm.

In sum, humanitarian organisations' distinct obligation to stay and remain engaged considers current aid recipients' excessive degree of vulnerability and humanitarian organisations' causal role in harm. The Distinct Dependence Account has significant normative value in helping humanitarian organisations navigate the most plausible moral judgement in the face of the Humanitarian Exit Dilemma.

The 'Distinct Obligation' to stay and remain engaged

A distinct obligation should generally take precedence over the duty to maximise aid efficacy when the two obligations conflict. This entails humanitarian organisations' staying and remaining engaged with current aid recipients even when they could do more good by withdrawing and reallocating their aid elsewhere.

Two arguments to ground this claim. Humanitarian organisations may do no wrong and are not morally blameworthy in causing the harm of unique dependency to current aid recipients. Nevertheless, they are liable for creating the harm of unique dependency because of their 'agent responsibility' (McMahan, 2009). Furthermore, although humanitarian organisations may not be culpable for the outcome of causing the harm of unique dependency to current aid recipients, they can be held responsible for their 'guidance control' capability. This is because humanitarian organisations have guidance control over whether they would get into a situation that would inevitably lead to a specific outcome (Fischer & Ravizza, 1998).

Agent responsibility

Recall the case of *Wrong Swimming Strokes*. You have significantly contributed to the drowning child's unique dependence by teaching her the wrong swimming strokes. Hence, you have a unique obligation to save her. In addition, you now have a distinct obligation to help her because you caused her incapacity. Causing harm to someone may be excused, depending on the particulars of the case. For example, causing harm to someone may be excused if you are unaware of its happening or cannot foresee it. Intuitively, you cannot be held responsible for what happens because of such an event. However, foreseeably causing harm to someone seems different. In *Wrong Swimming Strokes*, you actually can foresee that if you teach her how to swim, she will not learn other swimming strokes. Knowing this risk and still deciding to teach her, you are responsible for her well-being if the danger befalls her. This view of liability is that of agent responsibility (McMahan, 2009).

There are two possible ways of causing harm to the drowning child. You may cause harm to her by being reckless or negligent. For instance, you may fail to take reasonable precautions to prevent the harm of unique dependence from happening. This makes you culpable for causing harm. You may cause harm to her through no fault of your own. The harm may happen even though you take possible and reasonable precautions to avoid it, as in the case of *Wrong Swimming Strokes*. I focus on the latter case, assuming that a person can be liable only when he engages in a voluntary action that has a reasonably foreseeable risk of creating harm (McMahan, 2009).[4]

In the Humanitarian Exit Dilemma, humanitarian organisations either cause harm to current aid recipients recklessly or without being reckless. In cases where humanitarian organisations have caused the harm of unique dependence to current aid recipients through recklessness or negligence, humanitarian organisations are *culpable* for the harm. However, current aid recipients' unique dependence on aid may not always be caused by humanitarian organisations' reckless actions. Very often, it is also because of complex political disputes. Given this, one is inclined to think that humanitarian organisations should not be held responsible for contributing to current aid recipients' unique dependence on aid.

However, humanitarian organisations remain responsible (though not wrongfully) for causing the harm of unique dependence to current aid recipients, given that humanitarian organisations have chosen to engage in a specific action with a foreseeable risk of creating harm. In this context, humanitarian organisations have voluntarily assumed caring for current aid recipients. They are aware that their actions sometimes involve a reasonably foreseeable risk of creating the harm of unique dependence. Several cases discussed in both Chapter 2 and this chapter have shown that the Humanitarian Exit Dilemma can arise when humanitarian assistance undermines local capacities, resulting in the affected population's further dependence on external assistance. In this context, humanitarian organisations have acted in the knowledge that they are causing the harm of unique dependence to the affected population. In addition, humanitarian organisations have voluntarily imposed this harm on the affected population. In other words, the affected population is suffering the harm of unique dependence not because humanitarian organisations fail to prevent such harm from happening. Rather, they suffer harm because humanitarian organisations have turned the peril into actual harm by voluntarily carrying out humanitarian relief (Bohlen, 1908).

This is what has caused the current level of vulnerability. Merely contributing to current aid recipients' unique dependence on aid is insufficient for liability. Nevertheless, voluntarily contributing to current aid recipients' unique dependence, knowing that this action risks causing harm, is sufficient for liability. Liability, in this context, is to bear the costs of one's actions. Here, humanitarian organisations are required to do more to take care of those they voluntarily and knowingly harm. In this sense, humanitarian organisations have a greater reason to help those they have harmed than those not causally responsible for harming. The duty to assist those they have harmed is weightier simply because humanitarian organisations cause harm to affected populations.

Humanitarian organisations are responsible for significantly contributing to current aid recipients' unique dependence on aid, even if they are absolved of all culpability. This is because humanitarian organisations can control their contribution to the harm of unique dependence and know the outcome to which it contributes. Thus, humanitarian organisations should plausibly be held responsible for causing the harm of unique dependence to current aid recipients, even if they are not culpable for the harm caused. In sum, humanitarian organisations' causal responsibility and agent responsibility have held them responsible for causing the harm of unique dependence to current aid recipients even if the outcome is not in itself wrong.

Guidance control responsibility

The second argument is related to the first one. It focuses on voluntariness and a moral agent's capacity to choose a specific decision. It is widely assumed that one should only be held responsible for what is in her control, such as the harm she has caused due to recklessness or ignorance (Nagel, 1979). However, one's causal responsibility matters to the extent that one should be held responsible for what she has causally brought about (Williams, 1981; Wolf, 1990).

Common-sense morality suggests that we are responsible only for those things we can control. It is tempting to think that humanitarian organisations should not be held responsible. In fact, it may be intuitive to think that humanitarian organisations should only be responsible for the consequences within their control. This view, nevertheless, can be questioned. If humanitarian organisations are responsible only for what is within their control, other moral considerations are left unaccounted for. Humanitarian organisations should take responsibility for initiating a causal sequence that results in harmful consequences. This is especially the case when facing the Humanitarian Exit Dilemma.

Indeed, humanitarian organisations have the capacity to decide between remaining engaged with vulnerable aid recipients and withdrawing much-needed aid from them. When humanitarian resources have already caused the harm of unique dependence to victims of conflicts, humanitarian organisations should take extra care when deciding to withdraw. When facing the Humanitarian Exit Dilemma, humanitarian organisations decide whether to stay and remain engaged with those currently relying on their assistance or to withdraw and allocate humanitarian resources to other places or groups. In this sense, humanitarian organisations have control over the allocation of relief aid, which significantly affects the outcomes.[5]

We can flesh this out further by drawing on the conceptual framework of the moral agent's guidance control. Insofar as one is given the capacity to perform an act relevant to controlling the consequences and that act has led to harm, one can be held responsible for bringing about a consequence (Fischer & Ravizza, 1998). The core argument of this 'Guidance Control Account' is this: if you can exercise relevant capacities to act as you intend to, you have guidance control over your action. Consequently, if you are given the capacity to act in a certain way that can affect the outcome, and that outcome would have been different if you did *not* act, you have guidance control of that particular outcome. In short, if the given action affects the outcome, then you have guidance control of the outcome.

Imagine a scenario where humanitarian organisations are not culpable for the harm befalling the affected population, but they nevertheless play a causal role in bringing about such harm. Imagine another situation where humanitarian organisations are neither culpable nor casually responsible for the resulting harm. It is implausible to assume that humanitarian organisations are not responsible in any way in the first case. The outcome has happened because of their causal role in bringing about harm. Humanitarian organisations are *morally responsible* for causing the harm of unique dependence to current aid recipients, even if current aid recipients' unique dependence on aid is not intended. More specifically, humanitarian organisations can be held responsible because they are given the capacity to perform an act, in one way or another, that is under their control, and this act has affected the consequences (Fischer & Ravizza, 1998). In short, humanitarian organisations' causal role in bringing about a specific outcome through their particular action plausibly holds them responsible for the resulting outcome.

The point of humanitarian organisations' guidance control is not to discourage them from providing necessary assistance in the first place. Instead, it is given to demonstrate that, although difficult, humanitarian organisations have voluntarily chosen a specific act that they know will create aid recipients' unique dependence. Of course, humanitarian organisations do not entirely and solely cause current aid recipients' unique dependence on aid. Belligerents and the conflict itself are also part of the cause. However, the point is that humanitarian organisations can significantly contribute to the negative outcome of complicated disasters, which can make victims even more vulnerable. This recognition influences *whom* humanitarian organisations should aid. But it does not mean they should not provide aid *in the first place*.

In summary, the guidance control responsibility holds humanitarian organisations responsible for causing the harm of unique dependence to current aid recipients. This is because humanitarian organisations have control over whether they would contribute to aid recipients' state of unique dependence, even if they do not have control over the outcome itself. These arguments ground the claim that humanitarian organisations' distinct obligation is important, providing them with reasons to stay and counteracting their need to maximise harm-reduction.

Conclusion

Dependence on aid has long been viewed as extremely problematic. As seen in the example of Northern Mali and other examples discussed in Chapter 2, the affected population is often in a situation where local governments do not have adequate means to secure their lives, and belligerents have no intention of safeguarding their well-being. This has made the affected population's continued survival depend on humanitarian organisations' assistance and their assistance *alone*. If humanitarian organisations withdraw, the chances are that they will not survive. However, humanitarian organisations' assistance can cause harm to the affected population. Humanitarian assistance can undermine local coping strategies and encourage wartime economies, which results in the affected population's further dependence on aid (Anderson, 1999; Assal, 2008; Bartle, 2012; Christoplos, 2004; De Waal, 1997; Fineman, 2001; Richardson, 1997; Hassan, 1996; Knack, 2000; Marti, 2012; Prendergast, 1996; Stockton, 2003; Swift et al., 2002; Terry & Bianca, 1994).

Starting from debates surrounding aid recipients' dependence on aid, I first considered James' Unique Dependence Argument. I then built on James' Unique Dependence Argument to develop the Distinct Dependence Argument, which holds that humanitarian organisations have a distinct obligation to current aid recipients. Two reasons were provided to underpin the Distinct Dependence Argument. First, humanitarian organisations need to consider current aid recipients' vulnerability, given that they are *additionally* vulnerable compared to those who are not uniquely dependent on aid. Second, humanitarian organisations should be held responsible for *causing* the harm of unique dependence to current aid recipients. Humanitarian organisations' unique obligation, together with their causal role in causing harm to current aid recipients, generates humanitarian organisations' *distinct obligation*. This distinct obligation provides humanitarian organisations with morally sound justification to stay and remain engaged with current aid recipients.

The moral trade-off here is between two important considerations: humanitarian organisations' distinct obligation to stay and remain engaged with current aid recipients; and humanitarian organisations' duty to maximise aid utility and overall consequences. The Distinct Dependence Argument argues that humanitarian organisations should consider staying and remaining engaged with current aid recipients due to the following reasoning. Humanitarian organisations should prioritise assisting current aid recipients because they are made more vulnerable because of humanitarian organisations and are more vulnerable than other needy people. Therefore, the concern for current aid recipients' additional vulnerability should precede the concern for consequences. After all, the Distinct Dependence Argument rightly prioritises helping current aid recipients because they are more vulnerable due to the actions of humanitarian organisations that they can be held responsible for. These reasons justify making a distinct obligation weightier than a general duty to aid.

The Distinct Dependence Argument considers individuals' causal responsibility and the vulnerability of people affected, prioritising the most vulnerable and the neediest people. Rather than promoting the overall consequences through maximising aid efficacy and harm-reduction, the Distinct Dependence Argument relies on agent-centred reasons for providing aid. This is humanitarian organisations' causal responsibility for bringing about harm voluntarily and foreseeably.

In the next chapter, I consider humanitarian organisations' backwards-looking responsibility in misleading the affected populations to *expect* their continued engagement. I also discuss the affected population's trust in humanitarian organisations in extreme emergencies. I show that affected populations' reasonable expectations can be due to the *culpable* behaviour of humanitarian organisations. This chapter focused largely on non-culpable causal responsibility, but the next chapter considers the culpable causal responsibility of humanitarian organisations. This provides a further reason for humanitarian organisations to stay and remain engaged with the affected population.

Notes

1 Aid recipients' dependence on aid can, on occasion, be seen in a positive light, to the extent that aid saves lives. Aid dependency is considered negative "when current needs are met at the cost of reducing recipients' capacity

to meet their basic needs in the future without external assistance" (Lentz et al., 2005, p.10). However, insofar as aid recipients are severely in need of aid, "possibility of negative dependency should be a secondary concern" (Lentz et al., 2005, p.11).

2 The case of Bhutan will be presented in more detail in the next chapter. It is found that Bhutanese refugees expect to continue receiving external support from HAAs even if dependence on aid is not the only means for refugees in Bhutan to survive (Shrestha, 2011).

3 See Peter Singer's (1972, 1997) *Drowning Child* example in the 'Grounding affected populations' unique status of dependence section.

4 For reference, I use the case of the Wrong Swimming Strokes to make a similar point to Williams' (1981) case of the Lorry Drivers.

5 A far more radical view is that individuals can be responsible for what they have done, even if they do not have the ability to prevent something from happening. This is proposed by Harry G. Frankfurt (1969). I do not wish to engage with Frankfurt's line of reasoning.

References

Abiew, F. K. (2012). Humanitarian action under fire: Reflections on the role of NGOs in conflict and post-conflict situations. *International Peacekeeping, 19*(2), 203–216. https://doi.org/10.1080/13533312.2012.665698.

Anderson, M. B. (1999). Do no harm: How aid can support peace—or war. Lynne Rienner Publishers.

Assal, M. A. M. (2008). Is it the fault of NGOs alone? Aid and dependency in Eastern Sudan. *Sudan Working Paper, 5*(19), 1–19. Retrieved from https://www.cmi.no/publications/file/3067-is-it-the-fault-of-ngos-alone.pdf

Bartle, P. (2012). *The dependency syndrome.* Community Empowerment Collective. Retrieved from http://cec.vcn.bc.ca/cmp/modules/pd-dep.htm.

Bohlen, F. H. (1908). The moral duty to aid others as a basis of tort liability. I. *University of Pennsylvania Law Review and American Law Register, 56*(4), 217–244.

Christoplos, I. (2004). Out of step? Agricultural policy and Afghan livelihood. *Afghan Research and Evaluation Unit, Issue Paper Series,* 1–78.

De Waal, A. (1997). *Famine crimes: Politics and the disaster relief industry in Africa.* James Currey.

Fineman, M. A. (2001). Dependencies. In N. J. Hirschmann & U. Liebert (Eds.), *Women and welfare: Theory and practice in the United States and Europe* (pp. 23–38). Rutgers University Press.

Fischer, J. M., & Ravizza, M. (1998). *Responsibility and control: A theory of moral responsibility.* Cambridge University Press.

Frankfurt, H. G. (1969). Alternate possibilities and moral responsibility. *The Journal of Philosophy, 66*(23), 829–839.

Goodin, R. (1985). *Protecting the vulnerable.* University of Chicago Press.

Hammock, J., & Lautze, S. (1996). *Coping with crisis: Coping with aid.* Feinstein International Famine Centre.

Harvey, P., & Lind, J. (2005). *Dependency and humanitarian relief: A critical analysis.* HPG Research Report (p. 19).

Hassan, A. A. (1996). Beyond the locality: Urban centres, agricultural schemes, the state and NGOs. In L. Manger, H. A. E. Ati, S. Harir, K. Krzywinski, & O. R. Vetaas (Eds.), *Survival on meagre resources: Hadendowa pastoralism in the Red Sea hills* (pp. 103–119). The Nordic Africa Institute.

James, S. (2007). Good Samaritans, good humanitarians. *Journal of Applied Philosophy, 24*(3), 238–254. https://doi.org/ 10.1111/j.1468-5930.2007.00378.x

Jessen-Petersen, S. (2011). *Humanitarianism in crisis.* U.S. Institute of Peace.

Knack, S. (2000). *Aid dependence and the quality of governance: A cross-country empirical analysis.* World Bank.

Lentz, E. C., Barrett, C. B., & Hoddinott, J. (2005). Food aid dependency: Implications for emergency food security assessments. *IFPRI Discussion Paper, 12*(2), 1–50.

Marti, J. (2012). Addressing the critical humanitarian situation in northern Mali. *Humanitarian Exchange Magazine.* Retrieved from https://odihpn.org/magazine/addressing-the-critical-humanitarian-situation-in-northern-mali/

McMahan, J. (2009). *Killing in war.* Oxford University Press.

Nagel, T. (1979). *Moral luck. Mortal Questions.* New York: Cambridge University Press.

Prendergast, J. (1996). Frontline diplomacy. Humanitarian aid and conflict in Africa. *Disasters, 23*(1), 84–85. ISBN-13: 978-1555876968.

Richardson, L. (1997). *Feeding dependency, starving democracy: USAID policies in Haiti.* Grassroots International.

Shrestha, C. (2011). Power and politics in resettlement: A case study of Bhutanese refugees in the USA. *New Issues in Refugee Research, 208.* Retrieved from https://digitallibrary.un.org/record/721837?ln=en

Singer, P. (1972). Famine, affluence, and morality. *Philosophy & Public Affairs, 1*(3), 229–243. Retrieved from https://personal.lse.ac.uk/ robert49/teaching/mm/articles/Singer_1972Famine.pdf

Singer, P. (1997). The drowning child and the expanding circle. *New Internationalist, 289.* Retrieved from https://newint.org/features/1997/04/05/peter-singer-drowning-child-new internationalist

Stockton, N. (2003). Humanitarian values: Under Siege from geopolitics. In J. Walter (Ed.), *World disasters report 2003: Focus on ethics and aid.* Kumarian Press.

Swift, J., Barton, D., & Morton, J. (2002). *Drought management for pastoral livelihoods–policy guidelines for Kenya.* Natural Resources Institute Research, Advisory and Consultancy Projects.

Terry, F., & Bianca, C. (1994). *Message from MSF France coordinator in Ngara (Tanzania) to MSF France Programme manager.* Médecins Sans Frontières International. Retrieved from http://speakingout.msf.org/en/node/501

Väyrynen, R. (1999). More questions than answers: Dilemmas of humanitarian action. *Peace and Change, 24*(2), 172–196. https://doi.org/10.1111/0149-0508.00117

Williams, B. (1981). *Moral luck.* Cambridge University Press.

Wolf, S. (1990). *Freedom within reason.* New York: Oxford University Press.

5 Affected populations' reasonable expectations and promissory obligation

Introduction

This chapter considers the third central non-instrumental reason for humanitarian organisations to stay and remain engaged with those currently under the help of humanitarian organisations. I explore the normative strength of current aid recipients' reasonable expectations and humanitarian agencies' needs to fulfil these expectations. I call this the 'Reasonable Expectation Account' to protect aid recipients' welfare from harm resulting from their unfulfilled expectations. Two important doctrines, Doctrine (I) and Doctrine (II), are discussed in support of my Reasonable Expectation Account in addressing the Humanitarian Exit Dilemma: (i) humanitarian organisations have invited aid recipients to trust that they will take care of them through engaging in humanitarian relief missions voluntarily and knowingly, and hence (ii) a duty that demands humanitarian organisations fulfil current aid recipients' expectations is activated because humanitarian organisations are culpable for creating their reasonable expectations.

The Reasonable Expectation Account addresses the ethical predicament posed by the Humanitarian Exit Dilemma: should humanitarian organisations stay and remain engaged with those in need or withdraw their assistance to maximise the best outcome? In this context, the best outcome is the ability to exit and withdraw aid in order to reallocate aid to other places where more good can be achieved.

I begin by examining aid-expectations in the cases of Bhutan and Uganda. After discussing the possible types of aid-expectations, I ground the concept of reasonable expectations by providing distinctions between *reasonable expectations* and *promises*. To show how the normative concepts of reasonable expectations and trust are relevant to the Humanitarian Exit Dilemma, I discuss and elaborate on my 'Reasonable Expectation Account', building on

DOI: 10.4324/9781003306696-5

Thomas M. Scanlon (1990)'s 'Promissory Expectation Account'. The 'Reasonable Expectation Account' focuses specifically on aid recipients' and affected populations' reasonable expectations in extreme emergencies. Justifications that underpin the 'Reasonable Expectation Account' are given thereafter. Finally, I conclude that humanitarian organisations should take affected populations' trust and reasonable expectations seriously when deciding to withdraw or stay when facing the Humanitarian Exit Dilemma. This is important because humanitarian organisations may otherwise harm those they intend to assist and consequently undermine their welfare and rights.

Two clarifications should be made before proceeding. First, I focus only on cases where current aid recipients' dependence on aid has generated their reasonable expectations, such as the case of Uganda. Consequently, I do not explore cases where no reasonable expectations are generated. Also, aid dependency syndrome can vary in contexts and between individuals. Given this, targeting specific cases in which reasonable expectations are generated will help focus on the core argument of the chapter.

Second, I do not argue that humanitarian organisations have explicitly promised the affected population of the continued provision of aid. Nor do I argue that humanitarian organisations have explicitly agreed that they will continue to assist the affected population. Instead, I hold that humanitarian organisations have *implicitly* invited the affected population to trust and form expectations that they will continue to care for them, given that humanitarian organisations have taken up *caregiver roles* and *assumed caregiving tasks* over a period of time regularly on a voluntary basis. This point is further elaborated on in the later section of the chapter. Therefore, it is important to note that this chapter does not discuss classical promissory obligations, which involve actual promises or agreements. This chapter focuses specifically on concepts surrounding *reasonable expectations*.

However, there might be some exceptions where humanitarian organisations make explicit promises to the affected population. There was an incident in Ethiopia where a senior staff of humanitarian organisations promised a group of starving Somalians that food would be coming in two weeks, knowing well it was not. The senior staff justified his deed by saying, "it would give the Somalians hope" (Harrell-Bond, 2002, p.69). The senior staff had subjectively presumed the Somalians "had no other options but to wait" (Harrell-Bond, 2002, p.69). By misleading the Somalians to believe that food would come if they stayed in one place, the Somalians were eliminating all other options and "probably [were] condemning them to death by starvation" (Harrell-Bond, 2002, p.69). In situations like this, it should be clear that humanitarian organisations are culpable for making false promises that lead to Somalians' deaths. It is unclear whether situations like Harrell-Bond's example are commonly seen in the context of conflicts. Given the aim of this chapter, I assume that situations as such might happen but should not be taken as regular cases.

Affected populations' reasonable expectations

The affected population as aid recipients is likely to depend on humanitarian assistance and expect relief aid to continue due to the extreme destitution in conflicts and wars. More specifically, the affected population's expectations of humanitarian assistance often occur when aid resources become their last resort to sustain their basic livelihoods (Harvey & Lind, 2005; Marti, 2012). Therefore, there is a need to focus on the affected population's reasonable expectations in times of conflict.

In situations where people's lives are threatened and local capacities to cope with crises are overwhelmed, it is reasonable to appeal to humanitarian organisations for assistance. As indicated in the previous chapter, aid recipients' reliance on aid is associated with the following descriptions: aid creates dependency mentalities, undermines local economies, generates the continued need for humanitarian assistance, and traps aid dependents into chronic dependence on external assistance (Assal, 2008; Bartle, 2012; Christoplos, 2004; Devereux, 2004; De Waal, 1997; Fineman, 2001; Hassan, 1996; Knack, 2000; Swift et al., 2002). Under some conditions, aid recipients' unique dependence on aid can result in their forming reasonable expectations of humanitarian organisations' continued assistance.

The affected population's dependence on aid can be categorised into different levels. The affected population's expectations of relief aid and humanitarian assistance vary from context to context, depending heavily on how relief aid and humanitarian assistance function in conflicts. For example, if the affected population is able to rely on the regular delivery of aid, the chance of their expecting aid is higher. In addition, the affected population is more likely to form expectations of relief aid and humanitarian assistance when they understand what they are entitled to and when the aid is likely to be provided (Harvey & Lind, 2005). Based on these findings, it is suggested that the affected population is likely to form expectations of humanitarian organisations' assistance if they (1) deliver aid on a regular basis, (2) make the affected population aware of their entitlements, and (3) distribute resources fairly to the affected population (Harvey & Lind, 2005).

Although this is generally the case, the affected population likely forms expectations of aid even if they are not sure what they are entitled to or are uncertain when relief aid will be delivered. This is evident in the case of Uganda, where the affected population formed expectations of aid simply because aid remained the only means of survival and was provided regularly and constantly (Hovil, 2002). In light of this, there is a need to broaden the current criteria regarding the affected population's formation of expectations to include cases like Uganda. Below I present the case of Bhutan and the case of Uganda to show that current criteria, although reasonably attractive, may need to be broadened to cover all relevant types of aid-expectations relations.

Since the affected population can form expectations even if they are unaware of their entitlements or are uncertain of the allocation of aid, four types of 'aid-expectations relation' between the provision of aid and the formation of expectations can be identified.

i   First, the affected population is not dependent on aid and holds no expectations of aid. There is, therefore, no aid dependency and no expectations of aid.

ii Second, the affected population depends on aid but does not form expectations of aid, which leads to their dependency on aid without inducing expectations of aid.

iii Third, the affected population has formed expectations of aid even if they are not dependent on the aid provision. This creates a situation of no dependency on aid but expectations of aid.

iv Finally, the fourth type of aid-expectations relation can occur when the affected population is dependent on aid and also hold expectations of aid, hence dependency on aid with expectations of aid.

I only examine and discuss the third and the fourth types of aid-expectations relation, which are found in the cases of Bhutan and Uganda. This is because I focus specifically on cases where the affected population has formed their expectations of aid, as noted at the beginning. The case of Bhutan is the (iii) type of aid-expectations relation where the affected population does not depend on aid for their survival yet expects the continuation of aid. In contrast, the case of Uganda presents the (iv) type of aid-expectations relation where the affected population is dependent on aid and is also expecting aid because aid is the last resort for their survival.

Bhutan: no dependency on aid but holds expectations of aid

Bhutanese refugees in the 1990s are an example where the affected population is not dependent on aid for their survival but holds expectations of humanitarian organisations' continued assistance. Bhutanese refugees were found expecting support from humanitarian organisations "until they were completely independent and entirely self-sufficient" even if there were other means, in addition to aid, to sustain themselves (Shrestha, 2011, p.7). In fact, it was found that Bhutanese refugees were offered resettlement opportunities in various countries (Shrestha, 2011). Evidence of the affected population's expectations of aid without depending on aid was found, where they held humanitarian organisations responsible for their well-being and expected humanitarian organisations' continued assistance (Shrestha, 2011). Taking into account the case of Bhutan, it appears that the affected population can form expectations of humanitarian organisations' continued assistance without depending on aid for their survival.

Uganda: dependency on aid with expectations of aid

In contrast to Bhutan, the case of Uganda presents a situation where an extremely dependent affected population had neither capabilities nor resources to pursue any other means of survival but to depend entirely on humanitarian organisations' assistance. Refugees who lived in camps had to "live in relative isolation with limited choices", which undermined their ability "to sustain and improve their lives" (Hovil, 2002, p.23). It was found that Ugandan refugees living in camps were "totally dependent" to the extent that they had to depend on aid for survival (Hovil, 2002, p.13). Ugandan refugees living in camps were subjected to humanitarian organisations "to make decisions for them", which partially led them to form expectations of humanitarian organisations' continued assistance (Hovil, 2002, p.13). Finally, it was evident that "limited resources and choices available" to Ugandan refugees left them no choice but to stay in camps and to expect the continued provision of aid (Hovil, 2002, p.13).

The case of Uganda indicates that the affected population can form expectations of the continued provision of aid, even if they are unaware of what they are entitled to or uncertain when the aid will be allocated. In situations similar to the case of Uganda, aid dependents likely expect the continued provision of assistance simply because they have no choice but to depend on aid if they want to survive. The case of Uganda illustrates a specific context where aid dependents form expectations of aid mainly because of their extreme dependence on aid.

The affected populations can form aid-expectations, with or without dependence on aid. However, whether or not those expectations are reasonably formed is another question. Therefore, there is a need to show that current aid recipients hold *reasonable expectations* of humanitarian organisations' continued assistance and that this should influence humanitarian organisations' decision to stay.

Grounding reasonable expectations

There is a need to differentiate reasonable expectations from promises, given that reasonable expectations can be induced by other means than promising, and promising can fail to induce reasonable expectations.

Reasonable expectations and promising

I discriminate between reasonable expectations formed through individuals' plausible reasoning and promising. The latter are usually formed through one's explicitly promising, while the former is not. By explicitly promising people that I will perform a certain act, people come to expect the fulfilment of this act based on my promise. While promising can often create people's reasonable expectations, reasonable expectations can be created without promising.

The affected population holds reasonable expectations of humanitarian organisations' continued assistance not because humanitarian organisations have made a promise to them. Instead, the affected population has formed reasonable expectations of humanitarian organisations because of their certain behavioural tendencies and the affected population's trust in the nature of their works and their humanitarian characters. Reasonable expectations, therefore, can be created without promising. Below I show that promising does not necessarily lead people to form reasonable expectations.

To see the intuitive force of my statement, consider the following two thought experiment cases, *Refugee Fred* and *Refugee Jeff*.

Refugee Fred: Fred has formed a reasonable expectation that aid workers from Oxfam will take care of him. This is because Fred reasonably perceives that aid workers of Médecins Sans Frontières will fulfil their responsibility to care for him, given their caregiver roles. In addition, due to their behavioural tendencies to take care of him regularly over a period of time, Fred has reinforced his expectations of Médecins Sans Frontières aid workers' continued assistance.

Refugee Jeff: Jeff has formed a reasonable expectation that you will take care of him because you have explicitly promised him that you will do so. However, this is your first time taking care of Jeff; you have not done so before. Jeff has no idea whether you will act upon your promise, given that Jeff knows no relevant information about you. However, Jeff still holds a reasonable expectation that you will do so because of the promise.

In the case of Refugee Fred, it seems straightforward that Fred has formed a reasonable expectation that aid workers will take care of him because Fred has plausibly assumed that aid workers have to accomplish their caregiving tasks and fulfil their caregiver roles. Fred's expectation of assistance is further reinforced by the aid worker's long aiding history. It is in this situation that Fred forms his reasonable expectations of aid workers' continued assistance.

The case of Refugee Jeff presents a different scenario: Jeff has formed a reasonable expectation that you will take care of him because you have promised him. Jeff's reasonable expectation is formed simply through your promise rather than his perception of your role and task or your certain behavioural tendency. From these two cases, it is evident that you can create people's reasonable expectations without making an explicit promise or agreement to them. However, promising may not necessarily lead people to form reasonable expectations. That is to say, you can make a promise to people without creating reasonable expectations on their part.

Consider the third thought experiment case, the Disappointed Refugee Rob.[1]

Disappointed Refugee Rob: You have promised Rob that you will take care of him and intend to do so. Rob also knows you mean it when you make this promise to him. However, given your bad record of keeping a promise, Rob does not expect you to act upon your promise to take care of him as you promise.

In the case of Disappointed Refugee Rob, it seems clear that, although promising often creates people's reasonable expectations, it can sometimes create no expectations. In the example of Disappointed Refugee Rob, you do make a promise to Rob that you will take care of him. However, your promise does not create his reasonable expectation given various factors (in this example, your bad record). The case of Disappointed Refugee Rob hence shows that promising does not always incur one's reasonable expectation. Some promises bind even if the relevant agent does not expect your performance; there are also promises that bind where the relevant agent would be unharmed if you fail to act as she expects (Owens, 2012). Drawing on three thought experiment cases, I suggest three conclusions. First, reasonable expectations differ from promises. Second, although promising often creates people's reasonable expectations, it may not always be the case. Finally, although reasonable expectations and promising may induce the same type of expectations, the causal geneses of those expectations are different. While the former is a result of promising, the latter results from one's certain behavioural tendency and others' trust in one. The above three points are relevant to underpinning my Reasonable Expectation Account, given that the three points altogether serve as its basis.

Suppose my view that 'current aid recipients have formed reasonable expectations of humanitarian organisations' continued assistance' is sound. In that case, humanitarian organisations should be responsible for creating the affected population's reasonable expectations. Although humanitarian organisations do not explicitly promise the affected population, humanitarian organisations have nevertheless led them to form reasonable expectations of their continued assistance. After all, it is plausible for people whom you have led to form reasonable expectations to require you to make sure that they will not suffer the harm of unfulfilled expectations if you fail to perform as they reasonably expect.

The view that you are responsible for protecting those who hold reasonable expectations of you from a significant loss is proposed by Scanlon (1990). Scanlon famously argues that if you have led people to form reasonable expectations of your future conduct while fully aware that they wish to be assured of it, you are then obligated to act in accordance with their expectations in order to avoid causing the harm of unfulfilled expectations to them. I refer to this view as Scanlon's Promissory Expectation Account.[2]

Two expectation accounts applied in the Humanitarian Exit Dilemma

The Humanitarian Exit Dilemma often presents in conflicts and extreme emergencies where resources are scarce and not enough for all. In the face of the Humanitarian Exit Dilemma, humanitarian organisations are often forced to choose between staying and remaining engaged with those in need and withdrawing their assistance to allocate resources in some other places where the maximum outcome can be reached.

Scanlon's Promissory Expectation Account considers reasonable expectations arising through promising, which unfortunately does not capture the delicate relations between the aid givers and aid recipients and therefore cannot fully picture aid givers' duties and aid recipients' correlated rights. I, therefore, develop the Reasonable Expectation Account, where I reflect on reasonable expectations resulting from aid dependents' trust in humanitarian organisations' certain behavioural tendencies and the particular social role and duty they have assumed. The Reasonable Expectation Account, in this sense, captures and specifies what duty or responsibility humanitarian organisations should bear if they fail to exercise due care when creating aid dependents' expectations.

The Reasonable Expectation Account has three unique features. First, it distinguishes between the *culpable and non-culpable acts* of expectations-creating. This is done by differentiating negligence and recklessness involved in creating others' expectations. Second, it does not accept compensation as a sufficient means to protect others against the harm of unfulfilled expectations, given its *unsuitability* in conflicts and wars. Third, one's obligation to fulfil others' reasonable expectations remains, even if she unintentionally created the others' reasonable expectations.

This non-instrumental aspect of my Reasonable Expectation Account is critical when humanitarian organisations are in the midst of the Humanitarian Exit Dilemma, as it provides yet another morally weighty justification for humanitarian organisations to stay and remain engaged with those in need even in situations where they may prefer to withdraw and exit.

To show that Scanlon's Promissory Expectation Account cannot sufficiently safeguard aid recipients' welfare in extreme emergencies, I first examine the applicability of Scanlon's Promissory Expectation Account in protecting current aid recipients from the harm of unfulfilled expectations. The four pillar principles of Scanlon's Promissory Expectation Account are discussed, respectively.

The 'Promissory Expectation Account' and the four principles

The Promissory Expectation Account discusses the promising-based obligations incurred by people's reasonable expectation of your performance of a certain act. It holds that you are obligated to act if you have led people to form expectations about what you will do by your expression of intention and if their expectations are reassured by your expression of fulfilling their expectations. While your *expression of intention* to fulfil people's expectations will create their expectations about you, your *expression of fulfilling* their expectations will lead them to rely on and depend on you (Scanlon, 1990). Making people expect you to act, and rely on you to act, incurs an obligation for you to act as they expect. People may otherwise suffer from a significant loss if you fail to fulfil their expectations.

Principle not to deceive or manipulate others (Principle M)

Your obligation to fulfil people's expectations is initially derived from your basic moral obligation not to manipulate people unjustifiably. In other words, in order not to manipulate people wrongly, you have an obligation to act as people reasonably expect (if you have led them to form reasonable expectations about you). This view is named 'the principle not to deceive or manipulate others', Principle M.

However, if Principle M is all we have to say about what we owe to each other, people may suffer a loss in cases where no manipulation is involved.

In terms of protecting current aid recipients from the harm of unfulfilled expectations, if humanitarian organisations fail to act as aid recipients expect, Principle M is insufficient because it only considers cases where there are reciprocation relations between one agent and another. In most conflict settings, humanitarian organisations do not demand reciprocation from the affected population, not to mention the need for humanitarian organisations to manipulate or take advantage of them unjustly. If Principle M is followed, we would potentially allow humanitarian organisations to absolve themselves from protecting current aid recipients from the harm of unfulfilled expectations. Regardless of whether Principle M does require reciprocity, my general point is that reciprocity could not be suitable to ground the kind of obligation (the pro tanto duty) that stems from generating reasonable expectations, given that reciprocity might not be present in the Humanitarian Exit Dilemma.

To address situations like this, you should also exercise due care not to lead people to form reasonable expectations of you, especially when you know they will suffer a significant loss if you fail to act as they expect. If you fail to exercise due care not to lead people to form reasonable expectations of you, you have to take reasonable steps to protect them from significant loss. The former view is named the 'Principle of due care', Principle D, and the latter the 'Principle of loss prevention', Principle L. Principle D and Principle L are given to protect people like Jim against a significant loss if you fail to act as Jim expects.

Principle of due care (Principle D)

Principle D requires your avoidance of unjust manipulation and exercising due care not to lead people to form reasonable expectations about you. One must do so when there is a reason to believe that one would suffer a significant loss due to relying on those expectations (Scanlon, 1990). Specifically, Principle D is more demanding than Principle M because it includes vigilance against leading people to form reasonable expectations of you and avoiding intentionally manipulating others (Scanlon, 1990).

Although Principle D is more demanding, it may face the following problem: one cannot specify the precise extent of due care you are required to perform. Principle D can only loosely demand that you exercise due care not to lead people to form reasonable expectations of you. It cannot, for example, guide what you should do after you have led people to develop reasonable expectations of you.

In the context of humanitarian action, Principle D demands that humanitarian organisations avoid creating the affected population's reasonable expectations negligently. Under Principle D, humanitarian organisations are required to exercise due care not to lead the affected population to form reasonable expectations that they will continue to care for them, regardless of humanitarian organisations' intentions.

Consider the case of Bhutanese refugees again: they were led to form reasonable expectations that humanitarian organisations will continue to assist them given their long aiding history, the nature of their work, and their humanitarian characters. Given their reasonable expectations of humanitarian organisations' continued assistance, the Bhutanese refugees in question gave up alternative means to survive (in this case, resettlement). According to Principle D, humanitarian organisations are responsible for the harm of unfulfilled expectations that befalls Bhutanese refugees if they do not fulfil their reasonable expectations of the continuation of care. This is because humanitarian organisations should have exercised due care not to create Bhutanese refugees' reasonable expectations, but they failed to do so.

Although Principle D could generally hold humanitarian organisations responsible if they fail to act as the affected population expects, it does not specify *what kind of* obligation *or duty* humanitarian organisations are required to bear once they have created the affected population's reasonable expectations. Even if humanitarian organisations can be held responsible under Principle D, it is not clear what obligation they owe to aid recipients. Given this, the affected population as current aid recipients need more than Principle D to protect themselves from the harm of unfulfilled expectations.

To resolve this problem, 'the principle of loss prevention' (Principle L) is proposed, which states that once you have created people's reasonable expectations of you, you should be required to take reasonable steps to protect them from significant loss (Scanlon, 1990).

Principle of loss prevention (Principle L)

Principle L demands that you take reasonable steps to protect people against significant loss once you have intentionally or negligently led people to form reasonable expectations of you, knowing that they will suffer significant loss if you fail to act as they expect.

Although attractive, Principle L does not specify which actions you are required to take to protect people against significant loss. It can be a demand to fulfil people's reasonable expectations, it can be compensation for people's loss, but it can simply be a timely warning. A problem arises here: people cannot readily demand that you fulfil their expectations because Principle L allows you to give a timely warning, or compensation, to those who form reasonable expectations of you.

Although Principle L prevents humanitarian organisations from intentionally, negligently, or recklessly leading the affected population to form reasonable expectations of their continued care, Principle L cannot provide the assurance the affected population reasonably wants. In the context of conflict, the kind of expectations the affected population reasonably forms are humanitarian organisations' actual continued care rather than any other kind of loss prevention. Under Principle L, the affected population will still suffer the harm of unfulfilled expectations if humanitarian organisations fail to act as they expect.

Acknowledging that Principle L cannot give the kind of assurance that people reasonably want, the final principle of his Promissory Expectation Account, the 'principle of fidelity' (Principle F), is given. Principle F requires your actual fulfilment of people's reasonable expectations of you.

Principle of fidelity (Principle F)

According to Principle F, you are required to fulfil people's reasonable expectations of you, not only because you have voluntarily and intentionally led them to form expectations of you but also because your failure to do so will cause a significant loss. Your fulfilment of people's reasonable expectations is the only acceptable step you can take to protect them against significant loss. Both compensation and a timely warning are inadequate to protect them against significant loss: people's reasons to demand that you fulfil their reasonable expectations are sufficient to establish it as a binding duty unless it would be reasonable for you to reject Principle F (Scanlon, 1990).

Although appealing, affected populations as aid dependents can still suffer harm under Principle F. When facing the Humanitarian Exit Dilemma, humanitarian organisations need to be clear about what duty and obligation they owe to those they try to help and protect. However, Scanlon's Principle F tells us little about what aid recipients could do to demand humanitarian organisations of their continued engagement. Under Principle F, humanitarian organisations are allowed to create aid recipients' reasonable expectations without bearing any duties, as long as it is *unintentional*. This view is clearly at odds with the interests of the affected population.

Recall Principle F: you are demanded not to intentionally and voluntarily lead people to form reasonable expectations of you. Following this reasoning, you are free to create people's reasonable expectations so long as you do so *unintentionally*. Principle F hence cannot protect current aid recipients from humanitarian organisations' unintentional actions.

In summary, Principle M cannot protect the affected population from the harm of unfulfilled expectations if humanitarian organisations do not act as they expect because it does not consider cases where no reciprocal relations are formed. Principle D does not specify what kind of obligations or duties humanitarian organisations should bear once they have created the affected population's reasonable expectations. Unlike Principle D, Principle L can request humanitarian organisations to compensate the affected population's significant loss and to redress the harm of unfulfilled expectations if they fail to act as they expect. However, Principle L cannot specifically demand that humanitarian organisations fulfil the affected population's reasonable expectations. Finally, although Principle F can protect *some* victims from a significant loss, it cannot protect *all* victims from the harm of unfulfilled expectations because humanitarian organisations are excused for creating their expectations unintentionally.

Although helpful in illuminating the various considerations, the Promissory Expectation Account does not quite fit the kind of conflict situations I am interested in. I hence develop my own 'Reasonable Expectation Account' to apply in situations as such.

The 'Reasonable Expectation Account' and the two doctrines

When facing the Humanitarian Exit Dilemma, there is an appealing reason for humanitarian organisations to exit and withdraw their assistance from the affected population. Humanitarian organisations can reallocate and redistribute their resources to other conflict zones and disaster areas where more good can be done. For example, by exiting and withdrawing, humanitarian organisations may maximise harm-reduction and have an overall better outcome than staying and continuing the engagement with those currently relying on and depending on their help. However, all these utilitarian calculations and consequentialist considerations can sometimes be outweighed by other important normative reasons.

In this section, I show that the affected population's reasonable expectations and humanitarian organisations' need to fulfil these expectations have significant normative force against withdrawing aid when the Humanitarian Exit Dilemma occurs. The Reasonable Expectation Account I offer provides humanitarian organisations with a further non-instrumental reason to stay and remain engaged with current victims who depend on and rely on aid. I now explicate the two central Doctrines of the Reasonable Expectation Account. This holds the following:

Doctrine (I) and the normative basis of voluntary assumption of trust

Doctrine (I) considers the normative strength of the voluntary assumption of trust. You can invite people to trust you or lead people to trust that you will perform a certain action by voluntarily and knowingly taking up a certain role and assuming a certain task relevant to the fulfilment of that particular action.

This account of the 'Trust View' argues that when you promise people you will perform a certain act, you invite them to trust that you will perform it. To be more specific, if you have indicated to people your knowledge of the importance of the fulfilment of that act to them and your willingness to have them place their faith in your character regarding the fulfilment of that act, you have invited people to trust that you will perform a certain act (Friedrich & Southwood, 2008). If an invitation of trust is given to people by you, an obligation not to betray the trust you have invited in people is incurred (Friedrich & Southwood, 2008, 2011). This is what is referred to as one's duty of trust. If you fail to perform that certain acts and hence break your promise, you act wrongly towards the person to whom you made a promise because you fail to carry out your obligation not to betray people's trust in you (Friedrich & Southwood, 2008).

The Trust View account intends to ground the wrongness of originally breaking a promise. However, the notion of the Trust View can also be applied to explain the wrongness of failing in one's specific role. Be that a specific social role, a specific professional role, or a specific familial role. This claim lies in the following reasoning: when you voluntarily take up a certain role and knowingly assume a certain task, people can reasonably be led to trust you, in your fulfilment of that certain role and task. In other words, you have invited people to trust you (in fulfilling your role and task) because you have chosen to take up a specific role and assume a specific task for which people can reasonably hold you responsible. Intuitively, when you have invited others to place their trust in you, you are required to bear a duty not to disappoint or violate such trust. In that sense, if you have invited people to trust that you will perform a certain action, you are obliged to perform that action.

This is not to say that you will always incur people's trust in you if you have knowingly assumed a certain task and voluntarily taken up a certain role. In some scenarios, you may not incur people's trust in you. However, in some specific situations, such as where people have to rely heavily on your task and role, such as a doctor-patient situation or tutor-student situation, knowingly assuming a certain task and voluntarily taking up a certain role can lead to people's trust in you.

Intuitively, when we go to the hospital as patients, we trust that the doctor and the nurse will take good care of us and that they will be responsible for our well-being precisely because of the specific role and task they have assumed and taken up. The same is true for tutors. When we go to a tutorial or seminar as students, we trust that our tutors will teach us correct knowledge relevant to their expertise and that they will ensure all of us can understand the materials thoroughly. Although doctors or our tutors do not make an explicit promise to us, by assuming specific tasks and taking up specific roles, we trust them to fulfil their roles and task. To that extent, it seems plausible to hold that by voluntarily taking up certain roles and knowingly assuming certain tasks, you have invited people to trust you in fulfilling that role and task.

The normative basis of voluntary assumption of trust

You can invite people to trust that you will perform a certain act by indicating your knowledge of the act's importance and your willingness to have them believe that your character is relevant to fulfilling it. Notably, this action incurs a duty not to betray the trust you have invited (Friedrich & Southwood, 2008, 2011).

According to this view, humanitarian organisations invite current aid recipients to trust that they will continue to care for them. It is a reasonable claim, given that humanitarian organisations know that their continued presence and assistance are of great importance to the affected population. In addition, a humanitarian organisation also indicates its willingness to have an affected population place its faith in its character by voluntarily and knowingly engaging in a specific course of action for which the affected population can reasonably hold it responsible. Hence, humanitarian organisations invite affected populations to trust that they will care for them and not avail themselves of the option to betray their trust and abandon them. In this way, the failure of humanitarian organisations to respond to an affected population's trust is morally unacceptable and a violation of its *duty of trust*, which requires it not to betray the affected population.

Suppose that humanitarian organisations discover that a larger group of needy victims could be saved by reallocating aid to them after they have already invited current aid recipients to trust their continued assistance. Even if the organisations believe they should withdraw help from the current victims to assist the larger group of needy victims, their invitation to trust should alter whether they feel it is appropriate to do so; reallocating their assistance to the larger group of needy victims would mean disregarding such trust in a way that treats current aid recipients unfairly.

In addition, by inviting an affected population to trust them through their voluntary acts, a *self-assumed duty* not to violate this duty of trust is incurred. Therefore, humanitarian organisations not only owe a duty of trust to the affected population but also have a self-assumed duty not to violate this duty of trust.

As you self-assume a certain duty by an act of will, voluntarily assuming such a duty has a moral force. The validity of a self-assumed duty consists precisely in that it does not exist until you create it and in the fact that it is not universal; that is, it is owed only to a limited range of people (Hart, 1955). Further, this self-assumed duty is defined as a *special obligation*, reasoning that the duty does not exist until you create it (Goodin, 1985). It makes such a self-assumed (pro tanto) duty especially weighty because a self-assumed duty is not universal but assumed by you alone for a specific group of people (Hart, 1955).

Humanitarian organisations are bound with twofold duties: first, a duty of trust to the affected population; second, a self-assumed duty not to violate this duty of trust. Together, humanitarian organisations' duty of trust to an affected population and their self-assumed duty not to violate this duty of trust create a moral barrier to their failure to affirm the affected population's trust through continued assistance and engagement. As in the case of distinct dependence, what ultimately drives this account is the concept of *agent responsibility*. Humanitarian organisations knowingly and voluntarily take on trust relations, and these relations can negatively impact affected populations, even when they are not dependent, if the organisations make decisions based upon this reasonable expectation that harms them Humanitarian organisations, therefore, have weighty reasons to assist those they lead to form reasonable expectations.

Doctrine (II) and the normative basis of culpability and harm

Doctrine (II) is given to specify what obligation you should bear if you fail to exercise due care recklessly or negligently, leading people to expect you to perform a certain action. In other words, Doctrine (II) outlines the kind of obligation you are required to bear if you fail to exercise due care and have created other people's reasonable expectations because of your recklessness or negligence. In situations where you are acting recklessly and negligently in creating people's expectations (of your performing a certain act), you are *culpable* for leading them to expect that you will perform that certain act.

However, in situations where you are *not culpable* for leading people to expect that you will perform a certain act, you should bear a responsibility to compensate rather than a full duty to act as people expect. For instance, if you have created people's expectations through no fault of yours and have taken possible and reasonable precautions to avoid them, you are not culpable for creating their reasonable expectations. In situations like these, some degree of compensation may be considered a sufficient means to protect people's interests and redress their loss if you fail to act as they expect.

There are two reasons for this line of thought. First, intuitively, you should bear a less demanding responsibility (such as compensation) rather than a binding duty to fulfil their expectations in situations where you are not culpable for creating their expectations. Second, we can discriminate the kinds of duty or obligation you should plausibly bear between your *culpable act* and your *non-culpable act*. To be more specific, if we require you to bear the most stringent duty (the duty to fulfil people's expectations) in situations where you are not culpable for creating people's expectations, there will be no reasonable way for us to assign an even more stringent duty to you to properly address your culpability in creating people's expectations. Considering that such a distinction should be made and should remain, compensation may be plausibly considered a means to redress people's loss if you fail to act as they expect.

Of course, full compensation could be as costly as fulfilling people's expectations. To reiterate, my point is that humanitarian organisations may be required to fulfil some compensation, and this is typically less costly than fulfilling aid recipients' full expectations. In the Humanitarian Exit Dilemma, full or partial compensation may sometimes not be suitable since the victims may die if humanitarian organisations exit and withdraw, and so cannot be compensated.

Of course, there are situations where you can non-culpably lead people to expect that you will perform or follow a certain course of action. But here, I would like to dive deeper into situations where you fail to exercise due care, leading people to expect that you will perform or follow a certain course of action culpably. This view should be straightforward: if you could have taken reasonable precautions to avoid leading people to expect that you will perform a certain act but fail to do so, you are culpable for creating their expectations. In these situations, the only reasonable way for you to protect their interests is to fulfil their expectations. Compensation is insufficient to protect their interests in these situations.

Some may question: how about situations where you *unintentionally* neglect your responsibility to exercise due care to avoid creating people's expectations about you? In fact, the intention should not play a decisive role in this context. To be clear, unintentionally neglecting your responsibility to exercise due care is not, and should not be, considered morally the same as intentionally neglecting your responsibility—quite the reverse.

Intentionally neglecting your responsibility to avoid creating people's reasonable expectations is *morally worse* than unintentionally neglecting such responsibility. Even though this is the case, you may still be culpable for creating people's reasonable expectations when you neglect your responsibility to exercise due care unintentionally. This is because you still neglect and ignore your responsibility to exercise due care and not to create people's reasonable expectations. The fact that you have done so unintentionally cannot absolve you from the fact that you are culpable in creating people's expectations and are thus responsible for the subsequent harm of unfulfilled expectations that might befall them if you fail to act as they expect.

In most cases, humanitarian organisations do not intend to lead the affected population to expect their continued engagement. However, humanitarian organisations' culpable negligence in creating their expectations remains, regardless of humanitarian organisations' unintentional action in creating these expectations. Be it intentional or not, this reasoning cannot rightly absolve humanitarian organisations' culpability in failing to take reasonable precautions not to create the affected population's expectations.

The normative basis of culpability and harm

Humanitarian organisations can sometimes lead the affected population to form reasonable expectations of their continued engagement through recklessness or negligence. This is particularly prevalent in conflicts where insecurity is extremely high, and aid recipients' daily life is severely disrupted. In extreme emergencies like conflicts and wars, humanitarian organisations often do not take reasonable precautions to avoid leading the affected population to form reasonable expectations about their continued engagement when they know otherwise (recklessness) or should have known otherwise (negligence). Humanitarian organisations seldom, if never, take into account the affected population's reasonable expectations of their particular action. Also, humanitarian organisations often neglect that the particular roles and tasks they assume can affect the affected population's expectations of them.

Recall the case of Bhutanese refugees. As shown in the case of Bhutan, humanitarian organisations could have taken reasonable precautions not to lead Bhutanese refugees to expect humanitarian organisations' continued assistance. This could have been done by giving a reasonable, timely warning or adopting several safety measures. By acting negligently or recklessly, humanitarian organisations have created Bhutanese refugees' reasonable expectations and misled them into believing they will stay and remain engaged with the needy and vulnerable Bhutanese refugees. Humanitarian organisations' *culpable negligence* for creating Bhutanese refugees' expectations provided a morally weighty reason for them to act as Bhutanese refugees reasonably expected.

To that extent, where humanitarian organisations are found culpable for misleading the affected population to form reasonable expectations of their continued engagement, humanitarian organisations are required to bear an obligation to act as the affected population expects. This is to protect the needy and vulnerable aid recipients from suffering the harm of unfulfilled expectations. Also, this is to prevent humanitarian organisations from wrongly inflicting the harm of unfulfilled expectations on aid recipients if they fail to act as aid recipients expect. As such, current aid recipients' reasonable expectations of humanitarian organisations provide them with a morally significant reason to stay and remain engaged, especially when humanitarian organisations face a difficult Humanitarian Exit Dilemma and are considering whether or not to exit and withdraw.

We can also discuss it in terms of rights and the corresponding duties. Humanitarian organisations have a duty not to culpably mislead aid recipients to believe that they will stay and remain engaged. This is particularly the case where livelihoods are threatened, and resources are scarce. By negligently creating aid recipients' reasonable expectations, humanitarian organisations *wrong* them by not fulfilling aid recipients' reasonable expectations. Correspondingly, the affected population as current aid recipients have correlated rights against humanitarian organisations, which demand that humanitarian organisations fulfil their expectations.

This remains the case when humanitarian organisations face the Humanitarian Exit Dilemma. In this particular situation, humanitarian organisations *owe* it to the affected population to fulfil their expectations. To that extent, the affected population with rights against humanitarian organisations has a *special condition* to claim action from humanitarian organisations or demand their compliance to stay and remain engaged with them. It is a special condition that other victims lack. Even if humanitarian organisations have other important considerations, such as that they have to maximise aid utility and relocate aid to somewhere more victims can be helped, current aid recipients' special status in demanding humanitarian organisations' action still stands.

To sum up, Doctrine (I) argues that you have invited people to trust that you will perform a certain act when you knowingly assume a task and voluntarily take up a role for which people can hold you responsible. Given that you have invited people to trust, a duty not to betray that trust is thereby incurred. Doctrine (II) argues that if you fail to exercise due care to avoid creating people's expectations negligently or recklessly, you are culpable for creating people's reasonable expectations. Under this circumstance, the only sufficient means to protect people from the harm resulting from their unfulfilled expectations is to fulfil these expectations.

Together, Doctrine (I) and Doctrine (II) suffice and ground the duty of trust and shed light on the moral significance of an individual's moral culpability together, providing the justification that demands A do X.

Conclusion

The affected population's expectations of relief aid and humanitarian assistance vary from context to context. They are heavily associated with how aid and assistance function. When aid has been delivered for a period of time on a regular basis, the affected population who are currently under the help of humanitarian organisations can be led to form reasonable expectations of humanitarian organisations' continued engagement and the continued provision of relief aid. Being able to rely on aid makes it more likely that the affected population will form expectations of the continued provision of aid; however, it need not be the only means to create their expectations.

For instance, the affected population can be led to form reasonable expectations that humanitarian organisations will not ignore their expectations and will take care of them. This is the case given humanitarian organisations' certain behavioural tendencies and the affected population's trust in the nature of their works and characters. As humanitarian organisations are responsible for misleading the affected population to form certain expectations about them, they, too, are responsible for protecting the affected population from the harm resulting from their unmet expectations.

I discussed and examined the relations between aid recipients' expectations and humanitarian organisations' responsibilities and duties with Scanlon's Promissory Expectation Account. Although highly relevant, I showed that the Promissory Expectation Account could not sufficiently address difficult situations like conflicts and disasters. In light of this, I developed the Reasonable Expectation Account, which provides detailed justifications for humanitarian organisations to stay and remain engaged with those currently relying on and depending on their assistance. The Reasonable Expectation Account serves as a moral dogma in protecting the affected population from harm resulting from their unfulfilled expectations.

Based on Doctrine (I) of the Reasonable Expectation Account, the normative basis of voluntary assumption of trust, I show that a duty of trust that requires humanitarian organisations to fulfil aid-dependents' expectations is incurred. This is because humanitarian organisations have invited aid dependents to trust in their roles and characters. In addition, since humanitarian organisations have engaged in the humanitarian mission for a period of time and on a regular basis, the affected population has come to rely on this regularity and hence plan their lives around humanitarian organisations' behavioural tendencies. A duty of trust to perform as aid recipients expect is hence incurred. In addition, humanitarian organisations also have an additional self-assumed duty not to violate the duty of trust. This self-assumed duty is incurred due to humanitarian organisations' voluntarily and knowingly engaging in a specific course of action, where they know such behaviour will lead the affected population to form expectations about them.

According to Doctrine (II), the normative basis of culpability and harm, I show that an obligation that demands humanitarian organisations to stay and remain engaged with those in need is incurred if humanitarian organisations are culpable for leading them to expect their continued engagement. This is regardless of humanitarian organisations' intention: humanitarian organisations' obligation to fulfil the affected population's expectations remains, regardless of humanitarian organisations' intention. Humanitarian organisations have to fulfil aid recipients' expectations because humanitarian organisations are culpable for leading them to form these expectations in the first place.

The third non-instrumental aspect of addressing the Humanitarian Exit Dilemma is laid out and elaborated on in this chapter: humanitarian organisations should stay and remain engaged with the affected population rather than withdrawing assistance to maximise harm-reduction. The affected population's trust in humanitarian organisations, as well as humanitarian organisations' culpable negligence in leading the affected population to expect continued engagement, provide humanitarian organisations with ethically weighty justifications to stay and remain engaged with those in need.

In the next chapter, I combine aid dependents' reasonable expectations with those outlined in the previous two chapters (aid workers' special bonds with the aid dependents and their extreme vulnerability) to offer a complete Non-Consequentialist Approach to the Humanitarian Exit Dilemma.

Notes

1 The case of Disappointed Refugee Rob is similar to that of the Profligate Pal in Scanlon's Promises and Practices (Scanlon, 1990, p.217).
2 In the original text, Scanlon refers to his account as the 'expectational account of promissory obligation' (1990).

References

Assal, M. A. M. (2008). Is it the fault of NGOs alone? Aid and dependency in Eastern Sudan. *Sudan Working Paper, 5*, 19.
Bartle, P. (2012). *The dependency syndrome.* [Community Empowerment Collective]. Retrieved from https://cec.vcn.bc.ca/cmp/modules/pd-dep.htm
Christoplos, I. (2004). Out of step? Agricultural policy and Afghan livelihood. *Afghan Research and Evaluation Unit, Issue Paper Series*, 1–78.
Devereux, S. (2004). *Proceeding from UNOCHA '2005: Food security issues in Ethiopia: Comparisons and contrasts between lowland and highland areas.* Addis Ababa: Pastoralist Communication Initiative.
De Waal, A. (1997). *Famine crimes: Politics and the disaster relief industry in Africa.* Oxford: James Currey.
Fineman, M. A. (2001). Dependencies. In N. Hirschmann & U. Liebert (Eds.), *Women and welfare: Theory and practice in the United States and Europe* (pp. 23–38). New Brunswick, NJ: Rutgers University Press.
Friedrich, D., & Southwood, N. (2008). Promises beyond assurance. *Philosophical Studies, 144*(2), 261–280.
Friedrich, D., & Southwood, N. (2011). Promises and trust. In H. Sheinman (Ed.), *Promises and agreements: Philosophical essays* (pp. 277–294). Oxford: Oxford University Press.
Goodin, R. (1985). *Protecting the vulnerable.* Chicago, IL: University of Chicago Press.
Harrell-Bond, B. E. (2002). Can humanitarian work with refugees be humane? *Human Rights Quarterly, 24*(1), 51–85.
Hart, H. L. A. (1955). Are there any natural rights? *The Philosophical Review, 62*(2), 175–191.
Harvey, P., & Lind, J. (2005). *Dependency and humanitarian relief: A critical analysis.* London: Humanitarian Policy Group, Overseas Development Institute.
Hassan, A. A. (1996). Beyond the locality: Urban centres, agricultural schemes, the state and NGOs. In L. Manger, H. Abd el-Ati, S. Harir, K. Krzywinski & O. R. Vetaas (Eds.), *Survival on meagre resources: Hadendowa pastoralism in the Red Sea hills* (pp. 103–119). Uppsala: The Nordic Africa Institute.
Hovil, L. (2002). Free to stay, free to go? Movement, Seclusion and Integration of Refugees in Moyo District. *Refugee Law Project, 4*, 1–25.
Knack, S. (2000). *Aid dependence and the quality of governance: A cross-country empirical analysis.* Washington, DC: World Bank.

Marti, J. (2012). Addressing the critical humanitarian situation in northern Mali. *Humanitarian Exchange Magazine, 55.* Retrieved from http://www.odihpn.org/humanitarian-exchange-magazine

Owens, D. (2012). *Shaping the normative landscape.* Oxford: OUP, Oxford.

Scanlon, T. (1990). Promises and practices. *Philosophy and Public Affairs, 19*(3), 199–226.

Shrestha, C. (2011). *Power and politics in resettlement: a case study of Bhutanese refugees in the USA.* Geneva: UNHCR, Policy Development and Evaluation Service.

Swift, J., Barton, D., & Morton, J. (2002). Drought management for pastoral livelihoods–Policy guidelines for Kenya. Natural Resources Institute Research, Advisory and Consultancy Projects.

6 A normative account to address the Humanitarian Exit Dilemma

Introduction

Unsurprisingly, the trends in humanitarian discourse have always been dominated by arguments on aid effectiveness and efficiency, largely due to the belief that humanitarian organisations should maximise the best outcome in terms of harm-reduction. This requires humanitarian organisations to maximise the utility of humanitarian assistance and relief aid, including withdrawing assistance from the affected populations relying on aid if necessary. This phenomenon has developed due to the popularity of a simple account of consequentialism in resolving the Humanitarian Exit Dilemma. It is not a secret that humanitarian organisations often emphatically favour the welfare of the larger number of people over the smaller number because they adopt consequentialism in calculating costs and benefits when delivering aid. The scarcity of resources and the time limitation further reinforce the belief that maximising the utility of aid and resources cost-effectively is the best way to approach the situation. Conflicts often create 'mass-casualty triage' where limited resources and time make it impossible to assist everyone (Gross, 2009). This explains perfectly why humanitarian organisations often follow the utilitarian calculation, even at the expense of the most vulnerable affected population. The guiding principle of humanitarian action for humanitarian organisations is to spend aid on those who can be assisted and aided cheaply and save as many lives as possible.

There is no doubt that overall consequences matter and that consequentialism could as well be a way to resolve the Humanitarian Exit Dilemma. Indeed, at first glance, consequentialism appears to be intuitively attractive, given that it rightly captures one's intuition regarding the importance of maximising harm-reduction. However, as we have seen, further reflection upon the simple

DOI: 10.4324/9781003306696-6

account of consequentialism leads to doubts. Instead of being held as the one and only morally relevant value, achieving good consequences is only one value amongst all other substantive values. This chapter summarises the non-consequentialist arguments to resolve the Humanitarian Exit Dilemma, highlighting various elements from the preceding chapters and bringing them together in a complete normative account. This chapter weighs the importance of maximising the best outcome against the substantive value of (i) special relationships, (ii) distinct dependence, and (iii) reasonable expectations. This is the complete normative account of the Non-Consequentialist Approach that I propose to resolve the Humanitarian Exit Dilemma.

The aim of this chapter is threefold. First, to consider the weights of the three essential normative values discussed in the preceding chapters against the consequentialist account. Second, to propose modifications to current principles of humanitarian action for humanitarian organisations. Third, to provide implications for situations whenever and wherever Humanitarian Exit Dilemmas arise.

This chapter proceeds as follows. The next section will summarise the Non-Consequentialist Approach, which will be used to argue against the simple account of consequentialism on the maximisation of harm-reduction. The 'Priority of different normative values and the justification' section will consider the stringency of the four given values against each other in depth. This requires weighing the three non-consequentialist values (special relationships, distinct dependence, and reasonable expectations) against the concern for the overall consequence. In the 'Applying the Non-Consequentialist Approach in humanitarian action' section, I will discuss and show how the Non-Consequentialist Approach can enable humanitarian organisations to navigate their decisions in conflicts. In 'The modified account of principles of humanitarian action' section, I will present and propose the modified principles of humanitarian action for humanitarian organisations. The final section will give a conclusion, followed by the implications.

Summary of the Non-Consequentialist Approach

Three normative values of the Non-Consequentialist Approach were presented in Chapters 3, 4, and 5. They are (i) special relationships, (ii) distinct dependence, and (iii) reasonable expectations. Here I summarise the non-instrumental arguments relevant to upholding these three normative values, which ground the claim that humanitarian organisations should stay and remain engaged with the affected population. The normative arguments underpinning the three non-consequentialist values, in turn, are (i) special relationships' independent moral value; (ii) the affected population's additional vulnerability and humanitarian organisations' causal roles in causing harm to them; and (iii) humanitarian organisations' voluntary assumption of trust and their culpability in creating other reasonable expectations.

Special relationships

Special relationships have independent value and are viewed as having significant moral force. The value of special relationships stems from the importance of special relationships with humanitarian aid workers and their personal commitment to the affected population. Humanitarian aid workers' special relationships with those whom they have special relationships gave them weighty reasons to stay and remain engaged with the affected population. This, in turn, enables aid workers to view the affected population as having additional claims on their assistance, in contrast to other victims. These special relationships can also generate aid workers' associative duties to protect the affected population from severe harm, given that such relationships are akin to friendships, which have profound moral weight to the involved agents. Accordingly, humanitarian aid workers' special relationships with the affected population in conflict should not be dismissed or overlooked easily.

Distinct dependence

Current aid recipients' additional vulnerability and humanitarian organisations' causal role in causing affected populations' unique dependence on them should be considered seriously. Several cases showed that aid recipients are often uniquely dependent on humanitarian organisations for assistance in conflicts. This means that aid recipients' continued survival relies critically on humanitarian organisations' assistance and their assistance alone. In light of this, humanitarian organisations have a 'distinct obligation' to address the needs and interests of these aid recipients.

On top of that, humanitarian organisations can encourage wartime economies, reinforce the existing power imbalance, and severely undermine local coping strategies when delivering humanitarian assistance.

Humanitarian organisations thus should be held responsible for causing the situation of unique dependence. This remains the case even if humanitarian organisations are not culpable for causing the harm of unique dependence to current aid recipients. I invoked the notion of agent responsibility to justify this view, which contends that one can be held morally responsible for causing harm as long as one does so voluntarily and knowingly. To that extent, humanitarian organisations have weighty moral reasons to remain engaged with current aid recipients and keep their operations as reparation for the harm they have created.

Reasonable expectations

Current aid recipients' trust in humanitarian organisations and their reasonable expectations of humanitarian organisations' continued engagement are of moral significance. They should be taken into account when humanitarian organisations make a decision relevant to withdrawing or staying.

To begin, humanitarian organisations have taken up humanitarian caregiver roles and assumed caregiving tasks relevant to humanitarian organisations' staying and continued engagement that current aid recipients can reasonably hold humanitarian organisations responsible for. By inviting current aid recipients to trust, humanitarian organisations have a duty of trust not to disappoint current aid recipients' trust in their continued engagement. Humanitarian organisations have also self-assumed a duty not to violate the trust by voluntarily and knowingly engaging in a specific course of action. Therefore, humanitarian organisations' voluntary assumption of trust bars humanitarian organisations from withdrawing their assistance from current aid recipients.

In addition, humanitarian organisations have an obligation to fulfil current aid recipients' reasonable expectations, given that they are culpable for leading current aid recipients to form reasonable expectations of their continued engagement negligently or recklessly. If humanitarian organisations fail to fulfil current aid recipients' reasonable expectations, they will wrongly inflict the harm of unfulfilled expectations on them. To that end, humanitarian organisations should stay and remain engaged with current aid recipients due to their trust in humanitarian organisations, and humanitarian organisations' obligation to fulfil current aid recipients' reasonable expectations of their continued engagement.

The rejection of the simple account of consequentialism

Overall, the Non-Consequentialist Approach includes the values of special relationships, distinct dependence, and reasonable expectations in resolving the Humanitarian Exit Dilemma. By contrast, the simple account of consequentialism considers only the need to maximise harm-reduction. It calculates benefits and costs solely regarding maximising utility, efficacy, or cost. In doing so, the simple account of consequentialism overlooks other morally significant values.

It is important to consider consequences and their value when addressing the Humanitarian Exit Dilemma. Nevertheless, consequences are only one value amongst all other values. Humanitarian organisations should not simply suppose that the concern for consequences is all that should matter to them, given the diversity of their social relations and these social relations' "complex implications" for humanitarian organisations' duties and moral reasoning (Norman, 1995, p.103). Although humanitarian organisations have a duty to maximise harm-reduction to achieve as much good as possible and reduce as much harm as possible, such a duty should "occupy only a portion" of humanitarian organisations' moral reasoning (Norman, 1995, p.106). Such a portion should be limited, given that one has to take into account other "more specific responsibilities" that arise from her special standing to others, which also "compete for space" in one's life (Norman, 1995, p.106).

Therefore, humanitarian organisations should consider consequences as an important value but no more than an important value amongst all other values, for those other values also demand specific attention. In light of this, although important, the concern for the overall consequence should be compared with other morally important values. One should see consequences as a value that can be traded off or outweighed by other values. Only in so doing can one recognise and acknowledge the moral importance of consequences and take other morally significant values seriously. In addition, the simple account of consequentialism is mistaken, given that such an account tries to reduce all values, be that affections, commitments, feeling, and desires, to utilitarian considerations. The simple account of consequentialism cannot be satisfactory because it demands people "uniformly" think in a way that their actions will satisfy the requirements of consequentialism, which leaves no room for non-consequential interests that people genuinely care for (Williams, 1981, p.51). Furthermore, the simple account of consequentialism is incoherent, given that it discounts agent-centred thoughts and decisions and further disassociates one from her moral feeling (Williams, 1981). Undoubtedly, humanitarian organisations need to assist the affected populations. But humanitarian organisations need not think it morally preferable to assist a larger-sized affected population rather than a smaller-sized affected population. In other words, while the larger population may weigh with humanitarian organisations as a good reason to withdraw or reallocate their current projects, it is sometimes required to stay and remain engaged with the smaller population, which is currently receiving and depending on humanitarian organisations' assistance. This is because of the following reasoning: in some specific situations, the claims of those currently receiving aid may be greater than the claims of the larger population.

The smaller population (those current aid recipients) might have the right to demand continued engagement from humanitarian organisations. In contrast, the larger population cannot, given that humanitarian organisations are causally responsible for making current aid recipients additionally vulnerable. It can also be that the smaller number of current aid recipients can claim that humanitarian organisations will wrong them if assistance is withdrawn. In contrast, the larger population cannot because humanitarian organisations are culpable for leading current aid recipients to trust and expect humanitarian organisations' continued engagement. It can also be that current aid recipients have a cause for complaint, whereas the larger population cannot because current aid recipients stand in special relations with humanitarian aid workers. In such situations, one may as well reason that it is morally preferable for humanitarian organisations to save current aid recipients who are small in number rather than a larger population. The simple account of consequentialism is, therefore, implausible in this context.

Priority of different normative values and the justification

In contexts where one value always conflicts with another important value, there is a need for humanitarian organisations to justify their reasons for prioritising one value over another. This is because these substantive values, after all, cannot simply be implemented but need to be weighed against one another. This is especially true when humanitarian organisations face the Humanitarian Exit Dilemma. I have identified the values and offered some suggestions about their relative weight. I now consider in more detail the different weights that should be given to the four substantive values: distinct dependence, reasonable expectations, special relationships, and the overall consequences (conceived as maximising utility, efficacy, and minimising costs).

When the four given values conflict, three criteria should be followed:

i   Distinct dependence is the most important value that humanitarian organisations need to take into consideration;
ii   Special relationships should take precedence over the overall consequences and may take precedence over the normative value of reasonable expectations, although this is not always the case; and
iii   The value of reasonable expectations can sometimes give humanitarian organisations a weighty reason to counteract their need to maximise harm-reduction.

Below I show several diagrams to illustrate the stringency of each value. I give the example of drowning people to appeal to one's intuition in choosing one value over another when they conflict.

In Figure 6.1, I show that (i) distinct dependence is the most stringent value to be upheld. In Figure 6.2, I show that (ii) when special relationships conflict with reasonable expectations, special relationships may take precedence over reasonable expectations, although this is not absolutist. Finally, in Figure 6.3, I show that the value of (iii) reasonable expectations can provide one with sound justifications to counteract one's need to maximise the overall consequences (in terms of harm-reduction), depending on the given context.

Distinct dependence as the most stringent value

Imagine that you come across the following situation. You are by four pools: Pool A, Pool B, Pool C, and Pool D. As indicated in Figure 6.1, Pool A and Pool B contain the same number of drowning people (one person drowning in each pool) and the same number of capable swimmers available to save them (three capable swimmers by each pool). However, Pool D only has you available as a capable swimmer. Pool C has two drowning people. Each pool indicates different scenarios.

In Figure 6.1, you are facing the following situation. There is person A in Pool A, who claims your assistance because you are culpable for leading A to form reasonable expectations of your assistance. If you fail to come to A's aid, you will wrongly inflict the harm of unfulfilled expectations to A. In addition, you have invited A to trust you through your act of will. If you fail to assist A, you will violate the duty of

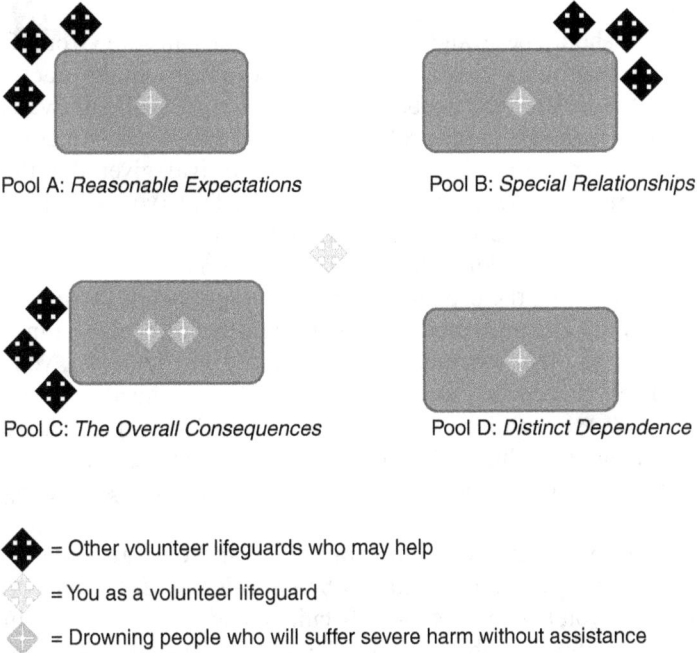

Pool A: *Reasonable Expectations*

Pool B: *Special Relationships*

Pool C: *The Overall Consequences*

Pool D: *Distinct Dependence*

= Other volunteer lifeguards who may help

= You as a volunteer lifeguard

= Drowning people who will suffer severe harm without assistance

Figure 6.1 Four Pools.

trust and your self-assumed duty not to violate the duty of trust. In Pool B, there is your close friend B, who is your close friend. Both you and B value this friendship a lot, and you both value it not merely for instrumental reasons. Therefore, you see B as having an additional claim for your assistance. There are then two people in Pool C; I call them 'Group C'. Group C are unknown to you but can be easily saved by you and others around the pool at once. Finally, there is person D drowning in Pool D. D is uniquely dependent on you mainly because of your causal contribution and partially because other lifeguards, for some reason (which need not entertain us here), cannot come to D's aid.

In situations like Figure 6.1, who ought you to help? Person A, who could hold you culpable if you fail to help; your close friend B, who has close ties with you; Group C, where two lives are at stake; or person D, who appears to be the most vulnerable amongst all people because of your causal contribution? I think our intuitions suggest that we should prioritise saving person D. (Note that it is assumed that there is a less than 50% chance that at least one of the bystanders to Pool C will jump in.)

The reason should be straightforward: while you can save Group C and preserve two human lives, three other lifeguards can do exactly the same. Due to this, the probability that Group C will survive is much higher in contrast to the probability that D will survive. In other words, Group C has a much higher chance of survival, given that the probable harm befalling Group C is divided by four (you and three other competent swimmers). Group C, after all, will only suffer severe harm if the four of you altogether, at the same time, fail to help. In contrast to Group C, the probable harm that might befall D is absolute and certain. The probable harm that might befall D also cannot be distributed to other swimmers. As illustrated in Figure 6.1, your help to D itself is necessary and sufficient for D's continued survival. In other words, your failure to come to D's aid is a complete cause of D's suffering severe harm. Given this reasoning, D is actually in a more vulnerable position than Group C (in terms of one's subjecting to harm).[1]

In addition to D's additional vulnerability, you should also bear in mind your causal contribution to D's being uniquely dependent on you. Although you may not be morally culpable for this, you have, in any event, causally contributed to D's being that dependent on you. Considering that D is additionally vulnerable compared to Group C and that you are responsible for causing D's unique dependence on your assistance, this appears to be the most binding obligation amongst your other duties. Your reason to come to D's aid is much weightier than your reason to come to person Group C's aid. Recall here that you voluntarily and knowingly cause D's unique dependence.

In a similar vein, although you are culpable for leading A to trust you and thus inducing A to form a reasonable expectation of your assistance, this concern is outweighed by the need to save the most vulnerable. This is because A, just like Group C, enjoys a relatively higher possibility of survival than person D. Although you will risk inflicting the harm of unfulfilled expectations on A wrongly (if you fail to act as A expects), you should still come to D's aid. After all, as noted above, you are causally responsible for causing D to be so vulnerable. Therefore, your reason to assist D can reasonably outweigh your reason to assist A. This is not to argue that your obligation to A can be dismissed. Nor does it argue that A's trust in you is not important. Instead, this shows that the value of reasonable expectations can be outweighed when compared with the normative weight of distinct dependence. My point is this: although you are culpable for leading A to expect that you will come to A's aid, whereas you are not culpable for causing D's unique dependency, your reason to assist D remains weightier.

By the same token, although close friend B has a close bond with you and she thus has an additional claim on your help, the fact that the chance of close friend B's survival is higher than D seems intuitively weightier than close friend B's claim against your prioritisation of assisting close friend B. Also, the fact that you have contributed to D's unique dependence has made you morally responsible for D's well-being. Although close friend B's additional claim for your help is valid, your distinct obligation to come to D's aid is still the most demanding, given that D is more likely to be subjected to harm than close friend B and that you contribute to D's situation. After all, the fact that close friend B has a higher chance of survival remains unshaken, which leaves close friend B in a comparatively better situation than D.

When the four values compete against each other, the value of distinct dependence should precede the three other values.

Special relationships as the second important value

After identifying that the value of distinct dependence should take precedence over the other three values when confronted with the Humanitarian Exit Dilemma, I now proceed to the following scenario, where the other three values clash, as illustrated in Figure 6.2. Again, the problem remains that each pool has a person or people in the group that require your assistance, and you only have time to choose one pool. You have an obligation to fulfil A's reasonable expectation of your assistance and a special obligation to your close friend B, and there are more people in Group C that you can save.

Person A, close friend B, and Group C have the same chance of survival as they have the same chance of being saved, as shown in Figure 6.2. In situations like this, your duty to assist those with whom you have special relationships might take precedence but not always. Your special relationship with your close friend B provides a weighty reason to reasonably counteract your other obligations (i.e. your other pro tanto duties). Hence, your special obligation to your close friend B may outweigh your obligation to fulfil person A's expectations. Your special obligation to your close friend B may also outweigh your general duty of assistance to Group C. The fact that you stand in a very special kind of relationship with close friend B seems intuitive to require that you prioritise the interests and needs of close friend B.

Pool A: *Reasonable Expectations*   Pool B: *Special Relationships*

Pool C: *The Overall Consequences*

 = Other volunteer lifeguards who may help

 = You as a volunteer lifeguard

 = Drowning people who will die without assistance

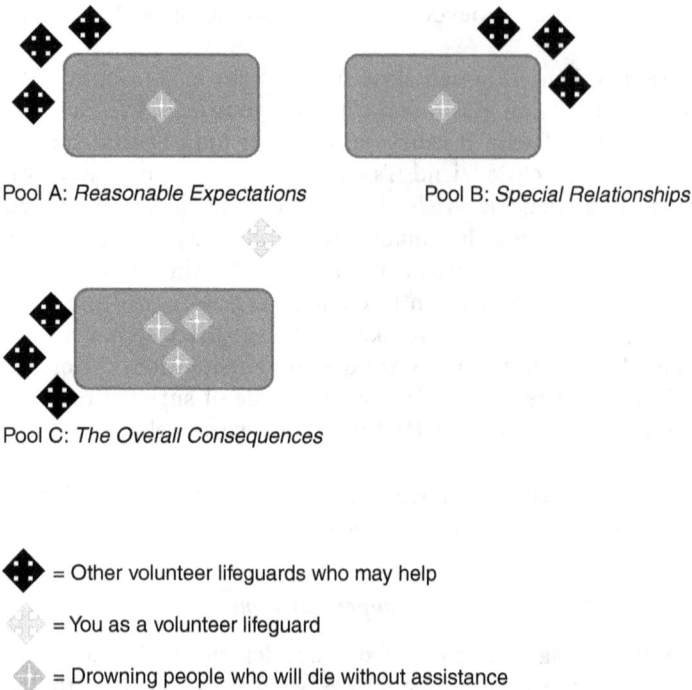

Figure 6.2 Three Pools.

Special relationships, to that extent, provide you with a weighty reason not to maximise the overall consequences.

However, it also seems plausible that your obligation to fulfil A's reasonable expectation could, on occasion, take precedence over your special obligation to your close friend B. What determines this are two factors that control the stringency of the given two obligations. First, the level of culpability (in terms of the moral wrongness) involved in creating A's reasonable expectation of your assistance (you are more culpable when the expectation being created is firmer; less culpable when it is less firm). Second, the degree of the special relationship between you and close friend B (i.e., stronger or weaker ties). That is to say, in situations where the degree of the special relationship is weak, whereas the level of culpability is high, your obligation to fulfil A's expectation is more stringent, and you should prioritise the considerations related to reasonable expectations.

Reasonable expectations may or may not outweigh the overall consequences

Inviting someone to trust you and misleading them to form a reasonable expectation of your certain behaviour may sometimes provide you with a weighty reason to counteract your need to maximise the overall consequences. As Figure 6.3 illustrates, you are standing by two pools, Pool A and Pool C. Person A trusts you and expects you to come to her aid. Moreover, you are culpable for leading her to form a reasonable expectation of your assistance. You, therefore, have an obligation to come to her aid. You will otherwise inflict the harm of an unfulfilled expectation on her if you fail to act as A expects, which is wrong. By contrast, Group C does not know you, and they are not led to trust or form reasonable expectations of you. Group C, nevertheless, is larger in number. In such a scenario, what ought you to do? Should you come to the aid of Group C, given that it appears to be the

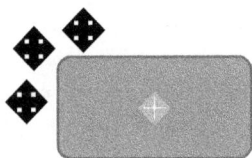

Pool A: *Reasonable Expectations*

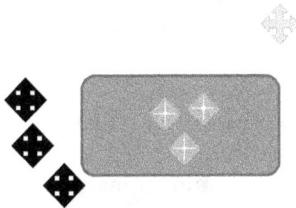

Pool C: *The Overall Consequences*

= Other volunteer lifeguards who may help

= You as a volunteer lifeguard

= Drowning people who will die without assistance

Figure 6.3 Two Pools.

best consequence, or should you assist person A, who has been led to form a reasonable expectation of your specific assistance due to your negligent and reckless action?

In this scenario, your reason to come to person A's aid is weightier than your reason to come to the aid of Group C. A has a greater claim on you. You only have a positive duty of assistance to come to the assistance of Group C. However, you have a specific obligation, a causal, or a remedial responsibility, to A, stemming from violating your negative duty not to inflict harm on A wrongly. In addition, your negative duties not to harm, in general, are held to be far weightier than your positive duties of assistance. So, your obligation to come to A's aid is more demanding in the given situation.

Note that although this is the case, it is worth reiterating that the importance of maximising the overall consequences may become more pressing in extreme cases. For instance, in cases where the decision must be made between assisting a small population (say, one needy victim) and a very large number of the affected population (say, 100,000 needy victims), the concern for consequences may outweigh your culpability.

After considering the priority of the four substantive values (although such a ranking is not set in stone), I now show how this priority ranking of the Non-Consequentialist Approach could come into play in conflicts.

Applying the Non-Consequentialist Approach in humanitarian action

This section has two aims: first, to show that the Non-Consequentialist Approach can indeed be applied to most conflicts; second, to show that the Non-Consequentialist Approach can equip humanitarian organisations with an overall sound moral framework to systematically and effectively address the Humanitarian Exit Dilemma and the ethical predicaments that surround it.

Several cases presented and discussed in the previous chapters of this book have shown that humanitarian organisations often need to justify their reasons for withdrawing or leaving due to the Humanitarian Exit Dilemma and its corresponding ethical predicaments. As shown in the cases of Uganda, Bhutan, and Northern Mali, reasonable expectations of humanitarian organisations' continued engagement and unique dependence upon humanitarian organisations' assistance are often seen amongst the affected population. These cases also indicate that humanitarian aid workers working for humanitarian organisations can form special relationships with the affected population and thereby commit themselves to specific affected populations. Although these given values need not always conflict with each other for the same humanitarian organisations at the same time at the same place, it is nevertheless often the case that humanitarian organisations will face this kind of conflicting situation when carrying out humanitarian operations.

It is often the case that affected populations currently receiving humanitarian organisations' assistance are uniquely dependent on humanitarian organisations, trusting them, holding reasonable expectations of their continued engagement, and having personal ties with humanitarian aid workers working for the organisations. This is especially likely to happen in the context of insecurity and violence. The reason is this: the affected population can be uniquely dependent on humanitarian organisations because they are often the only agencies and actors that can gain access to the conflict zone. Political disputes, as established in Chapter 2, prohibit the access of third parties such as state actors or governmental organisations. The affected population, in this context, can only rely on humanitarian organisations' assistance for survival. Furthermore, the affected populations are likely to place their trust in humanitarian organisations and hence form reasonable expectations of their continued engagement due to their humanitarian characters and caregiving roles. In addition, these reasonably formed expectations of humanitarian organisations can be further reinforced when humanitarian organisations deliver relief aid and humanitarian assistance over a long period of time on a regular basis.

Finally, the affected population can form close ties with humanitarian aid workers working in camps because of humanitarian organisations' long aiding history: those who work in camps to provide medical operations and vital goods to the affected population for a long period of time come to appreciate and value the friendship they have with the affected population. In these cases, humanitarian aid workers can develop a sense of solidarity with the affected population and regard their humanitarian operations as committed to them.

In this sense, humanitarian organisations are not simply facing the moral dilemma of whether to save the greater number or maximise the aid utility and effectiveness when deciding to withdraw or stay. Instead, humanitarian organisations face the moral dilemma of whether to trade-off three non-instrumental values for one instrumental value. Therefore, if humanitarian organisations are to justify their humanitarian action, they must first identify relevant normative values at stake. Only when humanitarian organisations can identify which value is competing and conflicting with which value can humanitarian organisations readily make a justifiable decision.

To help humanitarian organisations to make decisions in most conflicts, the Non-Consequentialist Approach also provides a plausible ranking of the four given values. In conflicts where upholding one specific non-instrumental value will conflict with the need to maximise harm-reduction, the Non-Consequentialist Approach proposes the following ranking: humanitarian organisations should uphold the value of distinct dependence. Suppose a given conflict presents a scenario where the different groups are equally dependent. In that case, humanitarian organisations should focus on the degree of special relationships (stronger or weaker) with whom they have formed special relationships. That is to say, if the degree of the special relationship is relatively strong, such as friendship, humanitarian organisations' reasons to stay and remain engaged with those whom they have special relationships can counteract humanitarian organisations' need to maximise harm-reduction. It may also provide humanitarian organisations with a weighty reason to overlook their obligations to another group who holds reasonable expectations of humanitarian organisations' assistance. Suppose the degree of special relationships is very weak. In that case, humanitarian organisations may want to fulfil their obligations to those whom humanitarian organisations have culpably led to form reasonable expectations of humanitarian organisations' continued engagement.

If a given conflict presents a scenario where the different groups have the same degree of special ties with humanitarian organisations, they then should consider the normative weight of the affected population's reasonable expectations of humanitarian organisations' assistance. At this point, humanitarian organisations should focus on their level of culpability (more or less) in creating the affected population's reasonable expectations. To be more specific, the firmer the reasonable expectations humanitarian organisations have induced, in general, the more culpable humanitarian organisations are; the more culpable humanitarian organisations are in creating the affected population's reasonable expectations, the more binding humanitarian organisations' reason is to stay and to remain engaged with the affected population.[2] Conversely, the lesser the humanitarian organisations' culpability in creating the affected population's reasonable expectations, the less demanding humanitarian organisations' reason is to stay and remain engaged with the affected population. In situations where the level of culpability is very trivial and the level of trust created is relatively low, humanitarian organisations should consider withdrawing from the affected population to maximise the overall consequences by maximising the utility of aid.

It seems clear then that the Non-Consequentialist Approach can help humanitarian organisations address the Humanitarian Exit Dilemma in a more comprehensive way, which accommodates not only humanitarian organisations' humanitarian ethics but also humanitarian organisations' concern for overall consequences. In the next section, I offer a modified set of principles of humanitarian action, which draws on this Non-Consequentialist Approach.

The modified account of principles of humanitarian action

Since humanitarian organisations have to identify different ways the Humanitarian Exit Dilemma can manifest in times of conflict and humanitarian organisations are agencies that endorse different values, norms, and principles, a modification of current principles of humanitarian action to accommodate these considerations is necessary. Below I show that both traditional and political principles of humanitarian action appear insufficient to help humanitarian organisations resolve the Humanitarian Exit Dilemma at stake.

Traditional principles of humanitarian action mainly focus on the humanitarian imperative (humanity), independence, impartiality, and neutrality (Barnett, 2011; Hoffman & Weiss, 2006; Minear & Weiss, 1993; Rieff, 2002). Although the humanitarian imperative and the notion of independence remain the most important principles of humanitarian action in humanitarian assistance operations, principles of impartiality and neutrality have attracted much criticism. As outlined in Chapter 2, while the operational principle of impartiality demands humanitarian organisations aid indiscriminately, the operational principle of neutrality demands humanitarian organisations stay neutral in the face of unjust events. Therefore, by committing to traditional principles of impartiality and neutrality, humanitarian organisations often enable belligerents and armed combatants to cause more harm. Traditional principles of humanitarian action hence often face difficulties in times of conflict.

However, theorists such as Mark Duffield (1996), Thomas Weiss (1999), Laura Hammond, and Hannah Vaughan-Lee (2012) propose to adopt different principles of humanitarian action. They propose to incorporate political engagement with the operational context of conflicts because "violent and protracted political crises [...] are now fashionable in the aid world" (Duffield, 1996, p.174). Given this, Hammond and Vaughan-Lee similarly argue that humanitarian assistance should not be about upholding principles of neutrality and impartiality but understanding "how humanitarian action is political in its own right" (2012, p.14). This leads to proposals for political operational principles that are partial and selective, as opposed to traditional operational principles of neutrality and impartiality. Political operational principles suggest that humanitarian organisations allocate aid based on who is being helped and act in ways that take sides with perceived just parties.

Although adopting political operational principles may help humanitarian organisations minimise the misappropriation of aid, such principles over-emphasise the need for political engagement when humanitarian organisations discharge humanitarian assistance. Political operational principles, too, face difficulties. Political operational principles can lead to overall counter-productive effects when humanitarian organisations deliver aid. On the one hand, political operational principles' emphasis on humanitarian assistance's political engagement can make armed combatants much more willing to harm humanitarian aid workers working in the field. This is because armed combatants often perceive and consider humanitarian organisations' humanitarian efforts as a tool used selectively by powerful external states.

In this sense, political operational principles of humanitarian action can create an adverse result and generate serious concern for humanitarian aid workers' safety (Abiew, 2012; Hammond & Vaughan-Lee, 2012; Jessen-Petersen, 2011). On the other hand, political operational principles can severely hinder humanitarian organisations from successfully performing their humanitarian missions. This is because belligerents are very likely to deny humanitarian organisations access to the affected population if they are perceived as partial or allied with the opposite side (Barnett, 2011; Barnett & Weiss, 2008; Hammond & Vaughan-Lee, 2012). In light of this, humanitarian organisations should reconsider politicising their humanitarian assistance, not only because political operations can impede aid delivery to the affected population but also because taking sides can risk costing the lives of those in need and humanitarian aid workers (Aneja, 2014; Barnett, 2011; Hopgood, 2008).

Regardless of the validity of traditional or political principles of humanitarian action, they are not very helpful regarding the specific Humanitarian Exit Dilemma that confronts humanitarian organisations. In other words, traditional or political principles of humanitarian action do not apply. Seeing that both traditional and political operational principles of humanitarian action cannot readily provide humanitarian organisations with sufficient guidance to address the Humanitarian Exit Dilemma, I provide a useful set of principles to guide responses to the Humanitarian Exit Dilemma facing humanitarian organisations. To properly address the Humanitarian Exit Dilemma that confronts humanitarian organisations, I incorporate four substantive values in principles of humanitarian action, which are values of distinct dependence, special relationships, reasonable expectations, and the overall consequences. Each of the values can provide humanitarian organisations with crucial moral guidance to address the Humanitarian Exit Dilemma. As discussed in preceding chapters, each value provides a weighty reason for humanitarian organisations to act, be that the vulnerability of the affected population, humanitarian aid workers' special ties with the affected population, or the affected population's trust and reasonable expectations of humanitarian organisations. See Table 6.1 for the description of each value.

Table 6.1 The four substantive values

Substantive value	Description of substantive values
1 Distinct Dependence	Considerations of different levels of *vulnerability* (the most and the least) amongst different groups and humanitarian organisations' *causal contribution* (more or less) to the affected population's state of vulnerability.
2 Special Relationships	Considerations of different degrees of *special ties* (stronger or weaker) between humanitarian aid workers of humanitarian organisations and the affected population and their relevant impact on aid workers' well-being and mental health (greater or lesser).
3 Reasonable Expectations	Considerations of different levels of humanitarian organisations' *culpability* (more or less) in creating the affected population's reasonable expectations and the affected population's trust (firmer or weaker) in humanitarian organisations' continued assistance.
4 The Overall Consequences	A consideration of different degrees of *consequences* (better or worse) regarding the overall lives being saved, the overall harm reduced, and the overall efficacy and utility of aid.

Below I propose a modified version of the principles of humanitarian action in armed conflict, which incorporates concerns for distinct dependence, special relationships, reasonable expectations, and the overall consequences into current principles of humanitarian action. To that extent, the modified version of the principles of humanitarian action takes into account both instrumental and non-instrumental values. Therefore, the aim is to suggest a set of modified principles of humanitarian action for humanitarian organisations. The proposed set of modified principles of humanitarian action takes into account both humanitarian values and accountable operational principles. To that extent, the modified principles of humanitarian action not only defend and uphold substantive humanitarian values but they also pay attention to good practice that considers the needs and interests of the affected population, such as transparency, accountability, and appropriateness. See Table 6.2 for the set of modified principles of humanitarian action.

Table 6.2 Modified principles of humanitarian action

Name	Modified principles of humanitarian action	Corresponding duty
1 Humanitarian imperative	**The Principle of Humanity** Humanitarian assistance should provide life-saving relief in the most imminent and life-threatening situations. It should affirm the view' that humanitarian assistance is concerned with the condition of individuals solely with regard to their status as human beings and should hence not affect by other considerations.	The general positive duty of assistance.
2 Distinct Dependence I	**The Principle of Vulnerability** Humanitarian assistance should correspond to the level of vulnerability. The more vulnerable victims of conflicts are, the more likely it is that they will encounter life-threatening suffering if this particular humanitarian organisation does not provide life-saving relief. It should affirm the view that humanitarian assistance is proportionate to need when assessing victims' vulnerability.	The unique obligation to assist those with whom one is in unique relations.

Name	Modified principles of humanitarian action	Corresponding duty
3 Distinct Dependence II	**The Principle of Causality** Humanitarian assistance should address the relevant negative causal consequences aid agencies impose on the affected population regarding aid-dependency syndrome. The more responsible humanitarian organisations are in making victims dependent on aid, the more demanding their causal responsibility is.	The distinct obligation to redress and rectify the harm created.
4 Security	**The Principle of Independence** Humanitarian assistance should refrain from connecting to any party with a stake in conflicts or advancing political agendas of any party. It should affirm the view that political engagement in aimed conflicts can pose severe threats to humanitarian aid workers.	A duty to be independent of any political actors.
5 Special Relationships	**The Principle of Appropriateness** Humanitarian assistance should affirm the value of humanitarian aid workers' agent-centred reasoning (such as local circumstances, aid workers' special commitments to victims of conflicts, and aid workers' standing in solidarity with victims of conflicts). Humanitarian assistance should take into consideration the moral importance of special relationships between aid workers and the affected population. If necessary, it requires that humanitarian organisations prioritise those with whom humanitarian aid workers have an affiliation and hence aid in a selective (as opposed to universal) way. This may demand humanitarian organisations reconsider the principle of impartiality and neutrality to stay neutral and aid indiscriminately.	The special obligation to those with whom one has a special relationship.

(Continued)

Name	Modified principles of humanitarian action	Corresponding duty
6 The Overall Consequences	**The Principle of Efficacy** Humanitarian assistance should be directed towards the relief of immediate disasters in the most efficient and cost-effective way. When there are no other morally relevant values that can outweigh its consequential benefits, an overall emphasis on the maximisation of aid utility is necessary.	The duty to maximise harm-reduction.
7 Reasonable Expectations I	**The Principle of Culpability** Humanitarian assistance should correspond to the level of humanitarian organisations' culpability, whenever it occurs. The more culpable humanitarian organisations are in failing to take reasonable precautions to avoid leading victims to expect that humanitarian organisations will continue to help them, the more demanding their duty is to address any resultant harm.	An obligation to act as one expects.
8 Reasonable Expectations II	**The Principle of Trust** Humanitarian assistance should sympathise with victims and understand their needs by answering to their interests and by not violating the duty of trust.	The duty of trust and the self-assumed duty not to violate the duty of trust.
9 Transparency	**The Principle of Accountability** Humanitarian assistance should be transparent, in order to respond to donors' requirements. However, humanitarian assistance also should be accountable to the affected population whom humanitarian organisations assist. The accountability to the latter should take precedence over all others.	The duty to donors and aid recipients.

The other principles are generally found in lists of standard operational principles for humanitarian action. I cannot justify them here, but they seem very commonsensical. For instance, it seems clear that humanitarian organisations should be transparent and avoid advancing the agendas of political actors. The proposed modified principles of humanitarian action are reasonable and sound.

While the principle of humanity, the principle of independence, the principle of appropriateness, the principle of efficacy, and the principle of accountability are discussed and proposed by several critical theorists such as Barnett (2011), Hammond (2008), Heyse (2006), Hoffman and Weiss (2006), Minear and Weiss (1993), Norman (1995), Stein (2008), and Weiss and Collins (2000), I propose to incorporate *the principle of vulnerability, the principle of causality, the principle of culpable negligence*, and *the principle of trust* to enrich the current principles of humanitarian action.[3]

To that extent, the proposed modified principles of humanitarian action not only maintain humanitarian organisations' core belief in the humanitarian imperative but also grant reasonable weight to the consideration of the overall consequences and other agent-neutral values. To that extent, the proposed modified principles of humanitarian action reflect both instrumental and intrinsic values of humanitarian assistance.

The proposed modified principles of humanitarian action do not face the same moral quandaries as traditional principles of impartiality and neutrality. More specifically, unlike the traditional principle of impartiality, the modified principles encourage humanitarian organisations and humanitarian aid workers working in the field to be partial and show solidarity with a specific group, given that they consider humanitarian aid workers' agent-centred reasons to assist that specific group. The modified principles also differ from the traditional principle of neutrality. Instead of asking humanitarian organisations to stay neutral, the modified principles deem it permissible or even necessary for humanitarian organisations to take sides, depending on the state of affairs. For example, in situations where humanitarian organisations are culpable for creating a specific group's reasonable expectations, humanitarian organisations should act partially or selectively and prioritise the interests and needs of those people. The proposed modified principles of humanitarian action also do not face the same problems as political operational principles. Contrary to political operational principles, the modified principles do not advocate political engagement or condemn a particular political standpoint. Instead, the modified principles only demand that humanitarian organisations weigh all relevant moral values against each other (regarding their demandingness) and make the most justifiable judgements themselves.

Conclusion

When providing humanitarian assistance and relief aid in the context of insecurity and violence, humanitarian organisations often do not have sufficient time to identify, evaluate, and prevent all potential threats to effective humanitarian actions (Heyse, 2006). This is even the case when humanitarian organisations are confronted with the Humanitarian Exit Dilemma. These threats are most likely beyond the control of humanitarian organisations and can hardly be prevented. If humanitarian organisations are to address all potential threats to effective humanitarian assistance, such as security concerns, donors' preferences, access problems, risks of complicity, and aid misappropriation, it will become very difficult for humanitarian organisations to make any decisions regarding aid provision at all. Instead, they should focus on choosing the most justified course of action within the epistemic and time constraints they are operating under. The principles that I have offered will help them do so.

It is also important to remember that humanitarian organisations are different agencies that "exhibit as many differences as similarities in ideology and approaches to the provision of assistance to vulnerable populations" despite their common goal of alleviating apparent suffering (Terry, 1999, p.4). Due to these differences, different humanitarian organisations often approach the Humanitarian Exit Dilemma differently. First, humanitarian organisations may differ in the importance they place on the proximity to state actors. Second, humanitarian organisations can differ in the degree of stringency they ascribe to operational principles of humanitarian action. Finally, humanitarian organisations can also differ in their pragmatic preference when delivering aid (Terry, 1999). Although different humanitarian organisations have different mandates, principles, and core values, all humanitarian organisations face conflicts between prioritizing the worst off and maximizing harm-reduction (Rubenstein, 2015).

To find a balance between prioritising the worst off and maximising harm-reduction, humanitarian organisations must recognise that the dominating ethos of their humanitarian efforts lies in "value rationality" rather than instrumental rationality (Weber, 1968, p.21). This is true because what locates the value of the humanitarian effort is its humane focus on "doing that [which is] good in itself" instead of "which is good for some other purpose" (Calhoun, 2008, p.23). Otherwise, humanitarian organisations' humanitarian efforts will be about counting "a calculus of bare life" and "the minimum of human existence", which represents nothing more than a "biological minimum" (Calhoun, 2008, p.5). It is, therefore, necessary for humanitarian organisations to steer their focus towards humanitarian ethics.

I believe the Non-Consequentialist Approach is preferable to the simple account of consequentialism because there exist other non-instrumental and independent values that humanitarian organisations may want to uphold and promote. To accommodate other morally important values, humanitarian organisations should adopt a Non-consequentialist Approach when delivering humanitarian assistance.

This is not to suggest that humanitarian organisations should not take into account the overall consequences. Instead of dismissing or overlooking the moral significance of consequences, I acknowledge that consequences indeed matter. I only wish to highlight the important implication that there exist other values humanitarian organisations should promote in addition to a concern for consequences. This requires humanitarian organisations to focus on how much weight to place on instrumental and non-instrumental values in a specific conflict context after determining which values and principles are relevant and valid. There is little doubt that providing relief aid and humanitarian assistance to the vulnerable population may risk supporting belligerents, producing more suffering, and being complicit in wrongdoings. However, there are various non-instrumental reasons for humanitarian organisations to stay, despite the aid's non-optimal outcome.

Implications

I will finish this chapter by highlighting some implications and extending the analysis more generally.

Humanitarian Exit Dilemma on disasters as a whole

More and more humanitarian crises and disasters are global, interactive, and complex. They may be caused or exacerbated by failed state contexts stemming from civil wars or be the outcome of protracted natural disasters. However, most crises and disasters are caused by a combination of both. Conflicts and wars may be the most complicated situations for humanitarian organisations to decide to withdraw or remain engaged in the crisis areas. However, the Humanitarian Exit

Dilemma is also relevant in other non-conflict contexts and can cause a pressing burden on humanitarian organisations.

Disasters severely disrupt the functioning of a community, and they often exceed the coping mechanism of the affected population and community. When allocating and delivering much-needed aid to the affected communities and the vulnerable victims of disasters, it requires more than a simple aid utilitarian ideology to do a good and 'humane' job. Humanitarian organisations need to go beyond maximising aid effectiveness where humanitarian assistance acts like goods providers in a capitalist market. It demands that humanitarian agencies approach the affected communities and vulnerable populations with care, empathy, and solidarity.

Natural and man-made disasters are often interrelated and correlated: protracted natural disasters often trigger political turmoil and economic collapse, leading to violent conflict that results in system failures. Weak institutional capacity, political instability, financial insecurity, massive population displacement, and fragile public infrastructure further escalate the pre-existing conflict, leading to a failed state and complex humanitarian crisis. With the restrained and limited humanitarian space and intensifying humanitarian crises, together with the sharp decrease in institutional donors' funding, the scale of humanitarian crises has outpaced the capacity of humanitarian agencies. The ethical quandary of the 'Humanitarian Exit Dilemma' is more relevant than ever in today's humanitarian crises.

On natural disasters

Disasters such as the tropical cyclone that hit Myanmar in 2008, the devastating earthquake that struck Haiti in 2010, and the catastrophic Typhoon Haiyan in the Philippines in 2013 all demonstrate the extreme scale of natural disasters. In 2010, a magnitude 7.0 earthquake struck Haiti and killed approximately 220,000 people, bringing immeasurable damage to infrastructure, and affecting nearly 3 million people. However, the catastrophic outcome was, in effect, the combination of the natural disasters and Haiti's existing socio-economic problems. The poorly regulated housing structures and overcrowding buildings, Haiti's political turmoil, and poverty have worsened and exacerbated the damage caused by the earthquake.

Typhoon Haiyan devastated Southeast Asia regions, particularly the Philippines, in 2013. It was one of the most powerful and deadliest storms to strike the Philippines: it destroyed more than 1 million homes and displaced about 4 million people. While relief aid and humanitarian organisations flooded in to provide assistance and much-needed help, local humanitarian organisations' role was largely ignored, resulting in poor integration of international and local relief efforts (The New Humanitarian, 2022). A need for humanitarian organisations to 'hand-over' the relief missions to the local civil societies and local humanitarian NGOs hence arise, which calls for the 'localisation' of humanitarian assistance.

On biological disasters

Biological disasters such as human-to-human virus transmission are not new. It dates back to the 1990s when the AIDS epidemic severely hit Africa. To date, millions of young people still cannot access the simple health services they need, especially in Eastern and Southern Africa (The New Humanitarian, 2022). Although the fight against AIDS has seen tremendous progress, with the gradual decrease in funding from institutional donors and state governments, the global health mission to eradicate AIDS by 2030 is under siege.

In 2013, we saw an outbreak of the Ebola virus epidemic in Western Africa. Ebola was one of the most widespread diseases in history, killing thousands of people and disrupting socio-economic conditions in Guinea, Liberia, and Sierra Leone. The Ebola outbreak in West Africa had spread from rural areas to densely populated urban spaces and infected people at an alarming speed. However, the international community was late in acting promptly to control the situation: the Ebola virus epidemic was only declared a public health emergency in late 2014, resulting from the late arrival of aid and a poor coordination system. Differing from the localisation problem mentioned above, here we saw the predicament of distrust between local and international NGOs: many humanitarian organisations, international as well as local, lacked the clinical expertise to respond to the Ebola outbreak adequately; and the situation was aggregated by ineffective communication and poor community engagement between the two (The New Humanitarian, 2022).

From 2019 until now, the COVID-19 coronavirus pandemic has spread worldwide and emerged as an ongoing global pandemic, continuing to affect and disrupt millions of people's lives globally. As of 13 October 2022, COVID-19 had recorded more than 623 million cases and 6.56 million confirmed deaths globally, making it one of the deadliest crises in history (The New Humanitarian, 2022).

The unprecedented crisis caused by COVID-19 has triggered severe social and economic disruption globally, leading to supply chain disruption, food insecurity, shortages in medical equipment, and crushing capacities of health facilities. Moreover, schools and universities were forced to close, enforcement of lockdown was in place, and fake news about COVID-19 had been spread through social media and digital platforms. Altogether, COVID-19 has led to intensified political tensions, unfair discrimination based on race and geography, and issues of health equality, which, at the same time, pose challenging questions on balancing between public health imperatives and individual rights to freedom.

Moreover, COVID-19 has forced local healthcare facilities and the humanitarian community to make difficult decisions regarding whom to save, as the daily death toll pressures overcrowded healthcare systems and outpaces the capacity of humanitarian organisations. The recent COVID-19 pandemic presents yet another relevant but different ethical challenge to the humanitarian community: humanitarian organisations are forced to have priority in mind when carrying out relief missions.

A Non-Consequentialist Approach in non-man-made disasters

For natural disasters, should humanitarian organisations focus on localising aid and hand over vital relief projects and missions to the local NGOs, inspired by the example of Typhoon Haiyan in the Philippines? As for biological disasters, should humanitarian organisations abort the mission and pull out of areas worst hit by the COVID-19 pandemic?

Two different but equally moral imperatives are at stake here in both examples. In the case of Typhoon Haiyan in the Philippines, we are confronted by the asymmetrical power relations between international humanitarian organisations and local NGOs. It is now widely assumed that it is not just recommended but a must to shift from foreign-dominated relief aid to localised funds. In the example of the COVID-19 pandemic, we face the ethical predicament of whether aid workers' safety can take priority over large numbers of vulnerable patients in urgent need. The general view is to pull the ground staff out due to the integrity and code of conduct to protect the aid workers.

On Typhoon Haiyan in the Philippines

When deciding how to hand over the relief programmes to the local NGOs, international humanitarian organisations need to analyse if the overall situation will bring more good than harm to the affected populations. In the case of Typhoon Haiyan in the Philippines, the priority is to assess the vulnerability of the victims in question, their ties with both international and local aid workers, as well as the trust incurred during the aiding missions. To apply the moral framework of the Non-Consequentialist Approach, before handing over the current relief missions to the local NGOs, international humanitarian organisations must make sure (i) victims of disasters are not worse off or made more vulnerable due to their exit, (ii) local NGOs are able to bond with the needed populations in a way that provides local NGOs with weighty reasons to take care of them with commitment even if international humanitarian organisations withdraw and exit the affected areas, and (iii) local NGOs should be able to handle and address trust incurred between the local populations and them and respond to their expectations and needs correspondingly.

Only when these three criteria are met can the 'hand-over' exit of international humanitarian organisations make moral sense. After all, a moral trade-off often needs to be made when facing the Humanitarian Exit Dilemma, whether are not they are local NGOs or international humanitarian organisations. Local NGOs, too, can face the pressure to pull out their aid workers from the disaster-struck areas if, by so doing, they can execute their reoccurs and funds more effectively in other areas in the country. Local NGOs, too, can mislead the affected population to form certain expectations about them but have to leave despite their unwillingness due to funding pressures or the aim to maximise the efficacy of aid. To hand-over or not to hand-over is not the question. The question should be 'whether handing over can make the affected people better off'.

On global pandemic COVID-19

Different crises pose unique dilemmas to humanitarian organisations. However, what remains the same is the need for humanitarian organisations to weigh up the relevant duties and obligations at stake to address the dilemma appropriately. In the case of COVID-19, humanitarian organisations face the 'pull-out dilemma' similar to the Humanitarian Exit Dilemma seen in most man-made disasters. The 'pull-out dilemma' is this: should humanitarian organisations stay and continue to respond to the needs of the affected population and community, or prioritise other equally important moral duties such as the safety of the aid workers?

With a decrease in available funds and the high-risk nature of COVID-19, discussions and debates surrounding the pull-out of ground staff for the sake of safety became prevalent. We must note that the duties at stake here are more complicated here: while humanitarian organisations have special duties to the affected populations when they decide to engage and intervene in the rescue missions, they, too, have duties to protect the lives of their employees, the aid workers in the field. When the two equally stringent special obligations collide and clash, humanitarian organisations should move on to other relevant and weighty duties to guide their decisions. Are they misleading the affected population's expectations and trust about their continued engagement? Are the affected populations worse off due to humanitarian organisations' intervention? Or are the affected populations uniquely dependent on a specific humanitarian organisation for help, meaning that they will certainly suffer imminent great harm if aid workers on the ground are pulled out and withdrawn? All these are fundamental questions we need to analyse and take into account when deciding whether or not to pull the ground staff out of the sites of the crises. If a humanitarian organisation is culpable and morally blame-worthy for creating certain expectations of the patients and, at the same time, remains the last resort for their survival, their duty to stay and remain engaged becomes extremely weighty: it may take precedence over the need to safeguard the security of aid workers.

There is no easy answer to the ethical quandary posed by any disaster, be them natural disasters, man-made disasters, or biological disasters. This is the feature and nature of any 'moral dilemma': some trade-off needs to be made, and these trade-offs usually involve a 'right versus right' decisions making process. It is right to localise the aid and empower the local community, local NGOs, and local civil societies. However, it is also right for international humanitarian organisations to stay and remain engaged if they can better safeguard the welfare and interests of affected populations. Similarly, it is right to take the safety and lives of aid workers on the ground seriously, and in some situations, it is even justified to leave those in need aside to protect the staff. On the contrary, in some other scenarios, it may be morally preferable for a humanitarian organisation to stay and continue its operation because it is accountable for creating patients' expectations and is the only available actor that is able to come to their aid.

The normative values this book brings in hence have their stake in humanitarian assistance outside of man-made disasters. The underlying principles for humanitarian organisations to consider when facing the Humanitarian Exit Dilemma in natural disasters or natural hazards remain similar though not identical.

Notes

1 This example rules out the risk of no one acting to assist Group C in Pool C. As mentioned at the beginning of the book, I only aim to argue against the simple account of consequentialism, which claims that one should always maximise the best outcome by promoting as many people's well-being as possible and reducing as much harm as possible, regardless of the probability.

2 There may be exceptions, but for simplicity's sake, I assume that the relationship between culpability and reasonable expectations is linear. I also assume that culpability and trust will generally go together, so when trust is engendered, the humanitarian organisations will also be culpable.

3 The principle of equality is not one of the modified principles of humanitarian action. Jennifer Rubenstein holds that equality is one of the most important values and argues that equalising outcomes amongst the different groups is "independently valuable" (2015, p.225). However, I believe the principle of equality should only be considered after humanitarian organisations address the four substantive values I suggested in the preceding chapters. This is not because the principle of equality is not important. Rather, this is because equality can only be upheld after humanitarian organisations have properly rectified and redressed the harm they inflict on the victims in question.

References

Abiew, F. K. (2012). Humanitarian action under fire: Reflections on the role of NGOs in conflict and post-conflict situations. *International Peacekeeping, 19*(2), 203–216.

Aneja, U. (2014). International NGOs and the implementation of the norm for need-based humanitarian assistance in Sri Lanka. In A. Betts & O. Phil (Eds.), *Implementation and world politics: How international norms change practice* (pp. 85–101). Oxford: Oxford University Press.

Barnett, M. (2011). *The empire of humanity: A history of humanitarianism.* Ithaca, NY: Cornell University Press.

Barnett, M., & Weiss, T. G. (2008). *Humanitarianism in question: Politics, power, ethics.* Ithaca, NY: Cornell University Press.

Calhoun, C. (2008). *The idea of emergency: Humanitarian action and global (dis)order.* Paper presented at the IILJ International Legal Theory Colloquium Spring 2009 Conference. New York.

Duffield, M. (1996). The symphony of the damned: Racial discourse, complex political emergencies and humanitarian aid. *Disasters, 20*(3), 173–193.

Gross, M. (2009). *Moral dilemmas of modern war: Torture, assassination, and blackmail in an age of Asymmetric Conflict.* Cambridge: Cambridge University Press. https://doi.org/10.1017/CBO9780511811562

Hammond, L. (2008). The power of holding humanitarianism hostage and the myth of protective principles. In M. Barnett & T. Weiss (Eds.),

Humanitarian in question: Politics, power, ethics (pp. 172–195). Ithaca, NY, London: Cornell University Press.

Hammond, L., & Vaughan-Lee, H. (2012). *Humanitarian space in Somalia: A scarce commodity.* HPG Working Paper.

Heyse, L. (2006). *Choosing the lesser evil: Understanding decision making in humanitarian aid NGOs.* Aldershot: Ashgate Publishing Limited.

Hoffman, P., & Weiss, T. G. (2006). *Sword & salve: Confronting new wars and humanitarian crises.* Lanham, MD: Rowman & Littlefield.

Hopgood, S. (2008). Saying no to Wal-Mart? Money and morality in professional humanitarianism. In M. Barnett & T. Weiss (Eds.), *Humanitarian in question: Politics, power, ethics* (pp. 73–97). London: Cornell University Press.

Jessen-Petersen, S. (2011). *Humanitarianism in crisis.* Washington, DC: U.S. Institute of Peace.

Minear, L., & Weiss, T. (1993). *Humanitarian action in times of war: A handbook for practitioners.* London: Lynne Rienner.

MSF Holland. (1994). *Breaking the cycle: MSF calls for action in the Rwandese refugee camps in Tanzania and Zaire.* MSF Holland Report. Retrieved from https://www.doctorswithoutborders.org/what-we-do/news-stories/research/breaking-cycle-calls-action-rwandese-refugee-camps-tanzania-and

Norman, R. (1995). *Ethics, killing & war.* Cambridge: Cambridge University Press.

Rieff, D. (2002). *A bed for the night: Humanitarianism in crisis.* London: Vintage.

Rubenstein, J. (2015). *Between Samaritans and States: The political ethics of humanitarian INGOs.* Oxford: Oxford University Press.

Stein, J. (2008). Humanitarian organizations: Accountable—Why, to whom, for what, and how? In M. Barnett & T. Weiss (Eds.), *Humanitarian in question: Politics, power, ethics* (pp. 124–142). Ithaca, NY, London: Cornell University Press.

Terry, F. (1999). *Reconstituting whose social order? NGOs in disrupted states.* Paper presented at the conference entitled From Civil Strife to Civil Society: Civil-Military Cooperation in Disrupted States, Canberra, Australia.

The New Humanitarian. (2022). *The 25 crises that shaped history.* Retrieved from https://www.thenewhumanitarian.org/Rethinking-humanitarianism-25-crises-shaped-history

Weber, M. (1968). *Economy and society: An outline of interpretative sociology* (Vol. 1). New York: Bedminster Press.

Weiss, T. G. (1999). Principles, politics, and humanitarian action. *Ethics and International Affairs, 13*, 1–22.

Weiss, T. G., & Collins, C. (2000). *Humanitarian challenges and intervention.* Boulder, CO: Westview Press.

Williams, B. (1981). *Moral luck.* Cambridge: Cambridge University Press.

Index

Note: **Bold** page numbers refer to tables and page numbers followed by "n" denote endnotes.

For Product Safety Concerns and Information please contact our EU
representative GPSR@taylorandfrancis.com
Taylor & Francis Verlag GmbH, Kaufingerstraße 24, 80331 München, Germany

www.ingramcontent.com/pod-product-compliance
Lightning Source LLC
Chambersburg PA
CBHW061746270326
41928CB00011B/2388